JfDI!
just do it

The
definitive
guide to
realising
your
dreams

JfDI!
just do it

Nicholas Bate

howtobooks

Published by How To Books Ltd,
3 Newtec Place, Magdalen Road,
Oxford OX4 1RE. United Kingdom.
Tel: (01865) 793806. Fax: (01865) 248780
email: info@howtobooks.co.uk
http://www.howtobooks.co.uk

First published 2005

British Library Cataloguing in Publication Data.
A catalogue record for this book is available from the British Library.

Cover design by Baseline Arts Ltd, Oxford

Produced for How To Books by Deer Park Productions
Typeset and design by Baseline Arts Ltd, Oxford
Printed and bound in Great Britain by Bell & Bain Ltd, Glasgow

NOTE: The material contained in this book is set out in good faith for general guidance and no
liability can be accepted for loss or expense incurred as a result of relying in particular
circumstances on statements made in this book. Laws and regulations are complex and liable to
change, and readers should check the current position with the relevant authorities before making
personal arrangements.

Contents

Chapter 1
Why is it going to work this time?

Welcome

J*f*DI!: Just Do It is the definitive guide for achieving your positive goals.
There are undoubtedly personal changes you want to make and at the
moment they are proving elusive: perhaps losing some weight,
possibly learning a language, maybe building your financial
independence. Possibly even more fundamentally, simply 'being
happy'. J*f*DI! will change that elusiveness, once and for all: absolutely,
definitely. Simply follow the straightforward strategies encompassed
by J*f*DI! in this book and the changes you desire will materialise.

Is it really going to be that easy?

Yes and no. It depends what you mean by easy! You'll need to put in
effort – you'd surely expect that, wouldn't you? And at times it will be
significant effort. But this guide will make sure you apply the effort in
the right way so that it isn't a struggle and consequently you get a
rapid return for your effort. Because once you do, your effort will
'snowball', you'll build momentum and a 'critical mass' or 'tipping
point' will be reached at which point success will be yours. So often,
effort is mis-placed, mis-guided or even makes your quest more
difficult. What <u>will</u> be easy is the strategy for success, the approach we
will take and the ease of application. I don't think any of us begrudge
effort when we see we are getting results; it's effort without
consequent success which can be dispiriting.

By the way, isn't there an 'f' in J*f*DI!?

There is and it is vital; we'll get to it in a while.

What evidence do you offer that it will work?

I look for results; I spend time with people who want effective, consistent results in business and to realise their dreams in their personal lives. It's my job. I run a consultancy (and have done so for 15 years) – Strategic Edge Ltd – whose simple vision is to 'enable individuals to realise and release their potential'. I work extensively with individuals and teams in organisations as similar and different as Microsoft, Marks & Spencer, Philips Electronics, Hudson Global, Intel... as well as many non-corporate organisations, even primary schools. We may use grand concepts such as organisational development and cultural shift, but in the end it's all about getting the individual to change. As one of our clients said a few years ago:

> *"In the area of Organisational Development, Strategic Edge has demonstrated cutting edge thinking. They pull together all the various strands of Personal development and illustrate how that impacts the development of the organisation. This is the first time I've seen tangible systems thinking delivered in a development programme. I believe that Strategic Edge is world class in this space."*

But it all starts on a personal level of course:

> *"If you are serious about work/life balance start with Personal Excellence from Strategic Edge."* – **Dr Philip Unwin**, Director, Wellness Centre, Microsoft

For our strategies to work at an organisational level, they must work at a personal level. So whether your interest is just that – personal – or whether it is to create a platform for cultural/corporate change, you're in the right place. And that's what this book will give you: *the strategies for change at a personal level.* For some of you it might seem surprising that personal work such as giving up smoking or managing debt is even discussed on such programmes – but think about it; once you can manage and achieve deep personal shifts in yourself then anything can be done. Fundamental changes such as:

Getting fit
Losing weight
Being happy
Getting promotion
Having balance: home and work
Enjoying life more
Starting a successful business
Giving up smoking
Writing a book
Successfully fighting your just cause
Resolving relationship conflict
Finding love
Living and working abroad
Making significant amounts of money
Learning to play a musical instrument
Worrying less
Inventing something
Raising a fantastic family
Starting a band
Giving your kids the education you want them to have
Travelling to your dream location
Being healthy again
Learning a language
Working part time

Amongst many others.

Every week via my programmes I see these fundamental changes happen and most importantly stick.

And just as importantly, it's worked for me. If you have had a chance to read my previous book, *Being the Best,* you'll know that I reached a stage where I had got my life into a total mess: seriously unwell, in debt, not enjoying my job...(do you want any more?). It needed turning around. These are the strategies I used and they will work for you.

> *"Whatever you can do, or dream you can, begin it! Boldness has genius, magic and power in it. Begin it now."* – **Goethe**

The structure of this handbook

In the next chapter we'll get down to work: there we're going to look immediately at the tools of JfDI! I want you to imagine that JfDI! is the overall toolbox; JfDI! is the label on the box. It's the box you reach for when you need some personal change(s) to occur. And of course in the box are the tools. Unlike many toolboxes, though, where tools are selected from a plentiful selection, we just have 12 special tools in our box; all of them are used and, further, they are used in a particular sequence, because each of them has a specific job to do on the route to creating the change we seek.

We're going to review the tools and thoroughly understand the job they each do, we can then apply those tools to seven application areas, seven desires. This initial brief period of review and understanding is critical; I say that because I know many of you (and I'm delighted that this is so!) will want to dive straight in and work on the specific change or changes which perhaps inspired you to read this book. But, please do remember that change is a subtle process and it's those very small points – applied with skill and tender, loving care – which make such a large difference to getting the change you seek. The difference between successful change and no change, between getting your desire and not getting your desire may well be in these subsequent early paragraphs, well away from the drama of your specific desire.

If it helps, the toolbox analogy continues to hold. In a carpenter's toolbox, there may be several hammers. To us, the non-expert, they all seem the same and when trying to put up a picture we bash in the nail using a hammer which is too heavy. We bend the nail, hit the wall and damage the plaster. Of course later we discover there is an alternative hammer with a lighter head, which does the job perfectly.

That's our goal: to do the job perfectly, to choose the correct tool for change, to become an expert at personal change. To ensure that personal change is no longer a struggle, but simply a process.

I have chosen seven 'applications' as being the ones which come up time and time again on my courses and during one-to-one coaching sessions:

Desire 1: **To lose weight, get fit, feel well and attractive**

The desire to be physically and mentally at our best. Of course once we start work on this desire, we'll need to get more precise. How much weight? How fit do you want to be? Why exactly do you want to lose weight? Looks? Health? Energy? All three? And what do you mean by attractive? But for the moment I will leave this desire as it is often expressed: a collection of physical improvements, which are of course often inter-dependent.

> *If you are seeking to widen your understanding of how change happens, this one will help you understand inter-related goals. Often we can't complete the change we seek because it is itself dependent upon another change being effected.*

Desire 2: **To give up smoking**

For many, this is the definitive test of their ability to get themselves to change! This one is pretty clear. The important aspect here is being able to achieve a sustained change, a change beyond the initial success which many people do achieve.

> *Again, if you are seeking a more general understanding of how personal change occurs, then this goal will in particular help you to understand the nature of the psychology of much personal change, i.e. that change is rarely purely logical. The strategy will be transferable to other addictions which are getting out of hand, from chocolate to coffee, from Chablis to cheese.*

Desire 3: **To write and publish a book**

Again, a clear desire. But two distinct stages are stated. Firstly writing the book and secondly getting it published; we will address both of them.

> *A bonus will be understanding the layers of desires. To run a marathon or to win the marathon?*

Desire 4: **To achieve financial independence**

This is of course a complex one. There are basic issues such as: how much money do you need to give you independence? And then there are tougher ones such as: why do you want it? The answer to that may not be as obvious as you think.

> *This is a great desire to study for really understanding how potentially confusing our desires can be and how easily seduced we can become by society's 'canned' messages.*

Desire 5: **To establish the career you want and/or the business of your dreams**

There are two separate desires here, both of which we will study.

> *This desire can be invaluable for understanding how the biggest blocker can be our own mindset and imagination.*

Desire 6: **To find and keep true love**

In a world of growing personal isolation, this apparently straightforward task is becoming an increasingly frustrated one. And in common with several of the desires we have mentioned, there is the question of maintaining it.

A desire which will help us illustrate that just when we thought this was not possible, it becomes so. And that even with something as apparently 'pure' and 'intangible' as 'love', we can create an approach which significantly heightens our chances of success.

Desire 7: **To be happy**

Ahh! The ultimate desire. And by the time we have developed the other six, we shall have had plenty to think about to prepare us for this one. And plenty of resources to make it happen.

One or more of these will, I am sure, be on your wish list. And the ones which aren't on our top list of seven – well, you will achieve all the know-how so that you can achieve them on your own.

"80% of success is turning up" – **Woody Allen**

"Don't let anyone dumb down your life" – **Nicholas Bate**

"Dream as if you will live forever,
 Live as if you'll die today" – **James Dean**

An introductory word about the 'f'

I did promise I would return to that temporarily neglected 'f'.

J*f*DI! is about 'doing it' – whatever 'it' is for you: losing weight, getting that relationship, building your own dream house. It is about no longer procrastinating, delaying, rationalising, excusing. It is about doing it; getting it done, achieving it, making it part of you, living and breathing it. And most importantly it is about realising that 'doing it' has two significant elements: the rational, logical side and the emotional, engaged (or not) side. Much personal change – getting fit, writing a book, achieving financial independence – is tackled, and discussed using ideas proposed from the logical side.

For example, The Sunday Papers arrive and contain an article on how to slim down for the beach this summer. We had been thinking about our body shape and think yes, it would be good to follow the ideas in the article. The article is oh, so logical. Why therefore, a week later, are we not doing anything about it? Because we have not addressed the other side: the *emotional* side, the *engagement* side, the *passionate* side.

Yes, we do want to be slimmer for the beach, but that decision has only happened at rational level, at a mental level. We haven't yet engaged our 'heart' and our 'gut' to support our head. The rational side to personal change is not enough; it is never enough. If it were, we'd all be perfectly fit, we'd have our financial futures planned to the last penny, we wouldn't have affairs which damage our family relationships. Why do many of us only address our health or a relationship when we have the crisis? Because by definition at that crisis point a whole new side of us becomes connected to the issue: we have become emotionally engaged and at last we do something about it. Why do many of us lose momentum after a while: our 'best-seller' gets neglected, the loft design is forgotten? Because the initial buzz we received has gone. We are no longer getting the emotional satisfaction of the results. We need to be emotional engaged, we need to feel committed. We need to feel I'm *fucking well* going to see this through. Strong, isn't it?

And that's why we use the word *fucking*. Just *fucking* Do It. It's strong. It's Anglo-Saxon. Its original sole meaning (before it also became a derogatory word) was indeed for sexual intercourse, probably one of the few processes nobody could approach with just pure intellect, however rational they are! But we have no doubt what it means. And interestingly even in this day and age it can cause a bit of a shock when we use it. But that's what the *f* is about: emotional engagement, together with the slight shock, the slight pause, the *pattern interrupt* to an old, no longer wanted behaviour. To finally do it this time.

JfDI! Just *fucking* Do It!

Yes, that *f* may only be 25% of the letter count of that word, but it's as much as 75% of the power.

So, bottom line, just what is JfDI!? JfDI! is our strategy for getting our dreams to be realised. It is about using the intellect of the brain coupled with the passion of the heart and the drive of the gut. It is about heart, gut and mind: all engaged. JfDI! is concerned with no longer fussing, no more melodrama. No more long conversations in the pub or during a dinner party conversation about why it hasn't happened. JfDI! is making it happen.

Heart and gut?

Traditionally, certainly romantically, our feeling side is expressed in the heart. And it is. But all those who have ever felt strongly about anything will know that we also feel things in our gut. We feel strength in our gut. We feel fear in our gut. That's why we will be working there, too.

It really will work this time

It really will work this time because we'll be answering all the tough questions. Ones such as:

- Why, even when we know we need to change and we want to change, do we find it hard to do so?

- Why, when we start to get the elusive change we seek, do we lose momentum?

- Why, when the change is clearly so important to us, do we put so little time into discerning the correct approach?

And all the other tough 'whys', too.

Top tips for getting the best from this book

We live in a busy, busy world. But it is still true that the best things in life still take a bit of time! So:

■ Slow down while working through this book and consider what you really do want and how specifically to apply the ideas to your situation.

■ Take notes and apply action points: get your own personal notebook and use it.

■ Or mark up this book with highlighters and yellow stickies.

■ Carry it with you at all times. *Read* and *read* and *study* and *study* and *think* and *think* and *discuss* and *discusss* and ACT and ACT.

■ If there is someone else who is interested in this stuff and you can buddy up with him or her, that'll make a good support system for you (both).

■ Do question everything of course. But all the ideas in this book, work, are tried and tested. So if you feel doubt or even cynicism at any stage, read a little further before abandoning your reading. You'll no doubt be aware that minds are like parachutes: they work best when they are open.

Finally

No significant change is ever easy. But giving *attention* to the change you want is a huge part of the process. You're doing that aspect already, so you're on the path.

Chapter 2
J*f*DI!: the tools

J*f*DI! is the definitive strategy for getting the personal change you seek. It works where other approaches fail because:

1. It accepts that for personal change, we must have intellectual understanding PLUS emotional engagement. For change we must *have* the evidence but we must want to act upon that evidence. We must have our:

   ■ brain engaged: we understand the relevant rational argumentation, the personal cost-benefit analysis and the return on our time/energy investment;

   ■ heart engaged: we feel that this is right and we are excited about getting on with it – we have a sense of passion;

   ■ gut engaged: we have a determined strength of purpose, we are managing any fear and we want it to happen.

2. It encourages a step-by-step brain- and time-friendly approach which gathers momentum, until a 'tipping point' or 'critical mass' is reached at which there is no return: the change is happening. All change can be broken down to a point at which it is sufficiently manageable so that 'change is ours!'

3. It recognises that we may *want* change but many of us feel we don't have the time to change.

4. It recognises that we all undergo change in a variety of ways and therefore there must be a collection of tactics in order to ensure we are sufficiently able to match to our personalities.

JfDI! will work on any aspect of personal change, assuming the person *wants* that change. In this work we are concerned with individuals who have recognised a change that they want and are having difficulty achieving it. Importantly the emphasis in this book is on the process of change rather than simply the content for change; this is not about changes you *ought* to make to make you a 'better' person. We'll leave you to decide which changes you want. The seven illustrative examples are certainly not selected as the 'best' ones to do, simply as the ones for which I am most commonly asked for help.

JfDI!: the approach

JfDI! is an overall approach or strategy which consists of three phases. Each phase has four identical levels of change, a total of 12 steps. If it helps, remember the toolbox? Well, it has three drawers and each drawer, four sections. Each of those 12 sections has a special tool. I'm keen that you learn these steps, that you know these stages, that you are expert with the tools: that they are at your fingertips. With that in mind I'll coach you as we study them to ensure you have got them. By learning them fully you engage with the process and then you have them ready for the future. So, let's learn them as we go by just doing a brief overview of the 12 steps and then we'll go into each step in more detail. After that we'll be ready to apply the process for real.

> The three overall phases are: Attention, Immersion and Momentum.

Attention

Attention is the first phase. Nothing happens without attention. Unless we actually give the change we desire attention: nothing! Obvious, really! Someone says to you that they would like financial independence and you ask them what they have done over the last month and they say 'Well, I've bought a few lottery tickets'. That's not attention, that's dreaming (you're more likely to be struck by lightening twice than to achieve financial independence through winning the lottery). A friend says they'd like to look more sexy. You then ask them what they have done and they've read a few articles at the hairdressers. That's not looking more sexy, that's filling your head with a lot of nonsense (generally, anyway)! Someone at a party says they'd like to have the fame of being the author of a best-selling novel. You ask them how their writing is going. They say they're still thinking. Yep, thinking is easy. But where's the action? Attention means we switch our brain to focus – and focus seriously on this desire. Our brain is very, very good at one thing at a time, but it's poor at multi-tasking (leave that to computers); let's make sure it's working on what we want.

When we give attention:

- We make a conscious decision to solve this issue, to achieve this personal change we are seeking. We prepare at mental level.
- We stop rationalising to ourselves and making up excuses about why we can't do it. We continue to prepare – profoundly – at mental level.
- We bring it to the forefront of our brain and our thinking: we visualise exactly what we want. We emotionally engage. We prepare at emotional level.
- We select the best strategy from the best source and then we implement it via a series of tactics. We prepare at strategic and tactical level.

Above all we move from vacuum to vision: we know where we're going and we know how we are going to get there.

For example, we decide to learn Italian. We make a specific decision that we want to be conversational in basic holiday Italian and we want to have a working vocabulary of 2000 words by summer of next year. We put aside that pathetic excuse which has begun to build up about being too busy and not being much of a linguist. We open our diary and we agree we will do 15 minutes every day: 10 mins of listening in the car on the way to work and 5 mins of vocabulary at lunchtime.

> We'll stop trying to work on it in the evenings, because that's not a
> good time for us. We decide that a good opening strategy would be to
> take a cheap flight to Rome and arrange via a language school to stay
> with a family for B&B and do a total immersion weekend.

Attention must happen. You know what it is like if you are talking to
someone but you haven't got his or her true attention. You go into
detail, but you don't get the acknowledgement from them that you
need. It's exactly the same with ourselves.

In a busy, busy world we must *get our own attention*.

Immersion

Immersion is the stage at which we put all other issues aside and focus
our maximum brain power and maximum emotional connection on
the change we want, thus giving ourselves maximum opportunity of
success by 'immersing' ourselves in the subject. In this phase we
'surround' ourselves with everything which will help us change and we
remove anything which will not. In this stage we reach a 'critical mass'
or 'tipping point' of progress. We have now got the change happening.

In this stage we recognise that a lot of the wiring in our brain and in
our muscle memory has been built up over a significant period of time
and therefore we will need to spend time to 're-wire' and develop new
muscle memories.

> For example, we decide our smoking has got to stop. And we decide
> we will *do nothing else* except give up smoking for the next week.
> Everything else can wait. After all, when we have given up smoking
> everything is going to be so much easier anyway. That way we can
> give all our energy, all our focus, to making it happen.

We can only get the change if we are completely thorough, if we give
the time to detox the old ideas, to re-wire, to re-build the new ideas.

Momentum

Momentum is our final phase in which the change is happening. We are losing weight and feeling a whole lot better. We are beginning to be able to chat in Italian. The first couple of chapters of our new detective novel are appearing. And we need to keep it going so that it is something which we 'live and breathe', something which is simply wired in to us. We need no special tricks or incentives to get us to keep this change happening. We need to ensure our original enthusiasm and momentum is not lost, that we keep our focus.

In this stage we must be honest and identify the blockers to our continued change: what has stopped us in the past perhaps? We particularly look at what will give us high pay-off results rapidly.

And in this final momentum phase we make the change a permanent part of how we work, something we live and breathe: an unconscious competence.

> For example, we join a weekly conversation class. And whatever, we always go. Sometimes we feel it is going well, sometimes we feel very frustrated because we are not progressing as quickly as we would like. Occasionally we decide not to go to the class any more. But whatever – assuming it is a good class – we keep on going. Because when we look back over the long-term, we see that we are making progress. And eventually we become students of the mantra of momentum: love the dip, love the plateau. More on that later!

You can easily remember the three overall phases by their initial letters: A, I, M, and the word **AIM** they create.

So, what were the three phases? That's right: **Attention, Immersion** and **Momentum**. Now as we mentioned, each phase has four levels. Let's rapidly overview those so that you understand how they work.

The four levels are the four at which change occurs: you already understand that the concept of change occurs both intellectually and emotionally. You also instinctively know that change occurs both through having an overall way or 'strategy' of doing it but also very importantly by implementing the details or 'tactics' of how to do it.

The four levels represent these four aspects of change. The four levels for each phase are always:

First level: what happens at BRAIN level? I.e. what happens at our logical/intellectual level? At this level we make a logical decision, we work things out in an if/then kind of way and a pros/cons way, e.g. how logically can I go about meeting more people so that I can discover the person of my dreams? If I place a 'lonely hearts' advert then this is likely to happen... How logically do we start building financial independence? Saving £15 per month at 4.55% interest per annum equals...

Second level: what happens at EMOTIONAL level? I.e. in our heart and in our gut. We know that change happens when we can get passion and engagement behind the change we are seeking, e.g. how we might overcome our fear of 'blind' dating, because we are going to need to if we want to dramatically increase the opportunities for meeting people. How do we get passionate about our writing so that we are willing to leap out of bed and start work on it, every day, every morning rain or shine?

Third level: what is our overall STRATEGY for success? This is our 'big picture' representation of what we want to do. E.g. it might be to simply multiply by ten the number of people we currently meet a month; surely we will meet someone we like that way.

Fourth level: what are the actual TACTICS for success? I.e. on a day-by-day even hour-by-hour level, what will we actually do? And how will we do it? Research safe on-line dating facilities? Research sensible speed-dating agencies? What will we actually do?

Got that? Excellent. Three phases: Attention, Immersion and Momentum. AIM. Each phase with the four levels. What happens at <u>Brain</u> level? What happens <u>Emotionally</u>? What is the <u>Strategy</u>? What are our <u>Tactics</u>? You can remember that by BEST. Easy so far?

AIM 4 BEST: a simple summary of the Michelangelo quote:

"The greatest danger for most of us is not that our aim is too high and we miss it, but that it is too low and we reach it." – **Michelangelo**

A point to note is that different people work in different ways and a consequence of that is you will tend to have more of an affinity for some of the levels than others, perhaps. Thus you may well feel that you see yourself more as a logical change agent than an emotional one. Or you may feel you're a 'nuts and bolts' person more than a visionary. This is fine and we certainly want you to work to your strengths. But also appreciate that you want to know why you haven't achieved the change you are seeking so far. And one reason will certainly be that you haven't worked on change at all levels. We will do so and that's one of the reasons change will work for you this time.

Now let's understand the tools more fully, getting more explicit about what happens in each of the four modules in each of the three phases.

Remember: there are three phases: Attention, Immersion and Momentum. And for each phase we must address what needs to happen at the four levels of: Brain level, Emotional level, Strategic level and Tactical level. *AIM 4 BEST.* For convenience we'll in future refer to the four levels by three phases as 12 steps.

And of course in the next chapter we will be applying these 12 steps generically. In the subsequent chapter we will start the specific desires.

Chapter 3
AIM 4 BEST

	Attention	Immersion	Momentum
Brain	●		
Emotion			
Strategy			
Tactics			

Step 1: Give ATTENTION at BRAIN level
Adjusting your mindset to support your change

The concept

You know that the quality of the software on your computer affects the results it will produce: you probably always try to get the best software you can afford and you regularly up-grade it if you feel new software will have advantages for you. Equally, you know how frustrating it can be if your software is corrupted by a virus: nothing is reliable, nothing is consistent and you certainly don't get any decent results.

That can happen to our personal software, our personal thinking. We all have the potential, generally speaking, to run excellent software, to run excellent thinking. But sometimes along the way we forget to upgrade our thinking in preparation for the new challenges which we are giving to it. Or sometimes it gets corrupted. Let's now re-load some decent software, some decent brainware. Because remember our software drives our behaviours which causes our results. One of the exciting things about our potential as human beings is we can choose our software; it just requires us to exercise our imagination and make that choice.

The way we think about a change, i.e. our mindset or our beliefs, are our 'personal code', our 'personal software'. That code, that software drives our behaviour which creates our results. For example, perhaps our old software was saying 'I'll never get a place at college to do that course' or 'there's no way someone like him would ever consider someone like me'. We can change that software to something more empowering such as 'I can get that place at college: I simply need to put the work in and get some coaching on my interview skills' or 'there's every reason why a guy like him might be attracted to someone such as me and here's why...' How about if your normal mindset with smoking is 'I'll give it a go, but I expect I'll fail long-term as I usually do' and we change that to 'I now know how I will make this a permanent personal change'.

Here are five excellent mindsets, five excellent beliefs, five excellent ways to give ATTENTION at BRAIN level in order to create personal change:

- **The past is history; the future I can design.** Whatever has happened in the past, it need not dictate the future, in particular your future, because you can learn from the past and change your approach in the future. This powerful mindset is not saying ignore or forget the past: certainly, learn from it. Which relationships didn't work for you? What areas of a business do you really not like running yourself? But then design afresh. This is the mindset of imagination and choice. Put aside unnecessary history. The fact that school set you back, that one of your parents was very constraining about your abilities. Put all of these points aside. Start *creating* your future.

- **I can.** Because you can, i.e. you physically can and you can mentally choose. When you say you can't get a loan for equipment for your planned business, you can. It's just that you haven't found the right person yet or you haven't made that one extra phone-call. This is a mindset of direction, of what is possible. You can. It does not matter that you are aged 57; you can start that business, despite some people's prejudices about 'older' people and the insensitive comment the bank manager made.

- **No failure, only feedback.** Because things won't always go to plan. When you decide to raise your standards you find that not every one is always supportive of you as you would like, that people let you down, that there are fundamental assumptions that you have made which are wrong. This is the mindset of 'kaizen' or continuous improvement. Success is dependent upon good judgement. Judgement is dependent upon experience. And experience is dependent upon bad judgement.

■ **There is a way.** Someone has a strategy for the change you want. This is the mindset of possibility and optimism. Not naïve optimism, not naïve 'positive thinking'. Simply resourcefulness. OK, so this is the situation I find myself in, what's the best route out?

■ **Love the dip and love the plateau.** Never ever give up on your dream. Along the way there will be set-backs, there will be times when you appear to be making no progress at all, there will be times when things appear to be getting worse. But you'll get there in the end. Love the plateau, love the dip (a tremendous quote, by the way, from George Leonard, author of *Mastery*).

An example

Tim had actually made the plunge and started a small business and was loving it. But as is often the way with a small business a lot of his cash flow was tied up with just a small number of clients. When one went bust, Tim had to stop trading too and he took it very personally and to heart and said he'd never try to run a business again.

Tim's great learning on the JfDI! workshop was:

■ **No failure, only feedback:** things will go wrong and sometimes badly wrong. But learn from those and keep learning.

■ **The past is history:** I can design the future: only use the past as a reference point. It need not necessarily predict the future unless you want it to.

For you: reflection and things to do

As you begin serious work on a personal change you require, bear in mind that your mindset – literally the way you think on the topic – will have a big impact: your mindset dictates your actions which in turn dictates your results. But your mindset is plastic: simply choose a more empowering one. Start practising to use any or all of the five empowering mindsets above.

NB's experiences

A helpful hint with new supportive mindsets is to 'act as if'. In other words, ask yourself, if I stopped seeing this as failure but as feedback how would I react? You'll find your mindset changes immediately. The more you do it, the more automatic it becomes.

Ifs & buts

But how do you 'take on' a new mindset?
You 'act as if'. For example, something doesn't go to plan. You feel you have failed. Using your notes you remind yourself of the empowering mindsets including 'no failure, only feedback'. How about if you 'acted as if' the failure you are currently experiencing were feedback, what would you do? How would you behave? Straightforward, isn't it?

And how do you get rid of limiting mindsets?
Notice that it is an unhelpful mindset. Once you have noticed it, destroy the evidence that apparently validates it. Thus 'many start-ups do not last any longer than three years'. Perhaps it is true, but many last a lot longer. Choose the latter mind-set for your business.

Is it really that simple?
How about if that was a new empowering belief that you took on board: that it is that easy! Seriously, I'm not being facetious. That is the approach you must take.

What creating a great mindset really means

- You will know how to give the change you crave, 100% attention.
- You will know how to stop 'trivial many' distractions.
- You will know how to 're-code' your brain for the results you want.

Step 2: Give ATTENTION at EMOTION level

Getting passionate and creating a vivid, explicit
mental model

	Attention	Immersion	Momentum
Brain	✔		
Emotion	●		
Strategy			
Tactics			

Concept

We have already acknowledged and it is
fundamental to our thinking in this guide that
any personal change needs both logical, mental
acceptance but also the passionate emotional engagement – the
engagement of heart and gut. In particular it is the emotional
engagement which creates the shift: when we are passionate about
something, it happens.

Passion drives change, but it is difficult to be passionate about
something about which you do not have clarity. You know what a clear
mental model does for you: absolute clarity about what is expected.
You know what full engagement does: nothing will stop you. Clarity
comes through creating a clear mental model. A clear mental model
acts as a beacon in the darkness; you know exactly what you are trying
to do, the point which you are trying to reach. But you say 'I know
what I want!' Well, perhaps. You say you want financial independence.
Well, how much? For what purpose? By what age? You say you want
to meet your true soul-mate? Well, what does that mean for your
search? We will look at how to create a 'sensory rich' mental model
which draws you into what is needed. By a sensory rich model we
mean something we can see, hear and feel. Something which is so
strong, it engages us at fundamental levels. E.g. how about if you
could hear the exact words you would use with the first journalists
interviewing you about your new book? No, really hear them: the
exact sound-bites. And if that sounds powerful and unlike anything
you've attempted before, that's why the change is definitely going to
happen this time!

How do we create a clear mental model? By building one within our
brain, by re-creating the three mental senses of seeing, hearing and
feeling that we would experience had we achieved what we were
looking for. We call this creating a Vivid, Explicit Mental Model. Vivid:

we can see it, hear it, feel it. Explicit: there is so much detail it is effectively real. Mental Model: it's in our head, ready to use. We'll call this a VEMM.

Here are the five steps of creating a VEMM:

1. Decide what you _want_, not what you don't want!
2. Now _assume_ you have achieved whatever it is you are looking for.
3. What are you _seeing_?
4. What are you _feeling_?
5. What are you _hearing_?

There are some important insights connected with each of the five steps:

1. Firstly, we very clearly focus on what we _want_, not what we _don't want_. It is very difficult to address a desire 'to not be so lazy' or 'to stop being miserable' or 'not delay on getting that first chapter written'. On the other hand, it is possible to address the need to: 'have sufficient energy to write 500 words every day of my new detective novel' or 'to be sufficiently resilient that I never let my work get me down'.
2. Secondly, we now use our amazing imagination, which for some of us has not had some really thorough use since we were a child. We imagine what it is like _now_ that we have achieved what we wanted. There _is_ our detective novel sitting there in a fantastic cover with our name clearly on the front. There we are at our desk every evening typing away and most evenings generating more than 1000 words rather than just 500 which was our initial target. There we are returning to our house, tired but feeling great after our 20 minute run. There we are walking hand-in-hand, our relationship re-invented...
3. We now create the VEMM in detail by asking, what are you seeing? And what else are you seeing?
4. And what are you feeling? And what else are you feeling?
5. And what are you hearing? And what else are you hearing?

Example

Lucy realised there were several reasons why she was not losing weight, but one important one was that she had no personal VEMM of how she wanted things to be. Her picture was always a 'morphed' picture of the models in the glossy magazines. And of course that could not be her: she knew most of those models starved themselves, stopped eating through using nicotine as an appetite suppressant, were airbrushed and about as real as a cartoon character. So her breakthrough came when through her VEMM work she decided that what she _really_ wanted was:

- To' walk taller'
- Lose 1kg over four months ready for the summer
- Change her hair style; to leave behind her 'college' days
- Improve her complexion
- Improve her body toning

Once she had visualised that, coupled with her empowering beliefs (step 1) she felt very excited because she knew it was possible, it was accessible.

Once you have got good at the basics of creating a VEMM – and you'll get very good, very quickly – then you can practice creating a super-VEMM. A super-VEMM is created by using our imagination to enhance the sensory nature of the image. Thus when you can see what you wish to create, how about if you improved the clarity or the colours of the image? Or how about if you had even more congratulatory voices speaking to yourself? It's straightforward and we will be exploring that process in detail in each of our seven desires.

For you: reflection and things to do
Early in the personal change process, ensure you have a clear VEMM that you are seeking:

Ensure that you are very specific about what you want:

- Not *I don't want to be so stressed* but I'd like to feel calm during the working day.
- Not *I don't want to work in large corporations*, but I'd like to feel part of a high energy team.

Build the detail in your sensory rich imagery

- Not just *I see me with lots of money* but I have a balance in my current account which is always around £50 and I pay my credit card bills on time...
- Not just *I see me briefing the team* but I gather the team around the whiteboard and I see me asking each member of the team for one of their achievements from the day before and one thing they would like help with...
- Not just *I see me with less weight* but I'm out shopping and I'm only buying my correct size, and they fit without squeeze and I have more selection of clothes...

NB's experiences

This is an excellent area to develop your expertise in creating personal change. For many, this step seems a bit odd and they are reluctant to try it. Or even worse, they say 'I tried it and it didn't work'. It will, but you must create the VEMM. If you have ever had an erotic thought you have used this process! We're simply harnessing it for a wider context!

Ifs & buts

How can I get past the fact that it just 'seems silly', when I 'imagine' having achieved the change?

That wouldn't be a limiting mindset, would it? Guess what? Back to step 1. Choose to withhold your disbelief and notice what happens.

What creating a VEMM really means

- You will know how to be confident of creating change.
- You will know how to overcome fear of change.
- You will know how to (re-)gain the passion for change.

Step 3: Give ATTENTION at STRATEGIC level
Selecting strategies to guarantee success

	Attention	Immersion	Momentum
Brain	✔		
Emotion	✔		
Strategy	●		
Tactics			

Concept

This might seem obvious, but to get the change we seek, we desire, we need to know how to do it. How do people write books? How do they produce all those words? 'The longest thing I wrote at college was 10,000 words and that took me most of a term'. And how do they make their characters so interesting? 'I just don't seem to notice all that stuff about other people?'

For the change you want there are some ways/techniques or strategies for getting them to happen. The important thing is to identify the correct one or ones. Assuming someone, somewhere has done what you want to do, there is strategy. And if no one has yet, then there is an opportunity for you to invent the strategy. There is always a strategy; how do we select the best one or a better one? We look for a strategy that gets results which are sustainable. For example, with losing weight there are tens of thousands of strategies, but there are only a few which will give you sustainable weight loss.

Here are some important points about strategies:
- A strategy is a sequence of things which must be done for success. E.g. when losing weight one must also carry out exercise. When investing in the stock market, only invest in companies which you know something about. Both of those latter elements might be considered successful elements in an overall success strategy.
- An expert at something doesn't necessarily know the strategy he/she uses; in fact some experts *don't want* to analyse how they do it for fear of losing their ability. Be aware therefore that although it is tempting to go to the expert we will generally need to complement that with other information.
- We can get strategies from books, courses, research on the internet and other sources, as well as from the expert him/herself. Our simple calibration for an appropriate strategy is that it gets the results that we seek.

- Being able to select the correct strategy is of course highly dependent upon a clear VEMM: we must match the VEMM to the strategy.

Example

Susan's strategy for gaining early financial independence, of dabbling in the stock market, was probably simply too high a risk for her. It could be a successful strategy, but probably only for a few people. And specifically probably not for her. Her strategy was not correct for her VEMM.

For you: reflection and things to do

Before undergoing any personal change, writing a book, losing weight, down-sizing to Wales, raising money for the village hall, ask:

- What specific strategy do I need? As always, what exactly am I trying to achieve?
- Where can I get that strategy? Is there a book I have read which is good? Is there someone I can ask? Remember when asking someone they might initially say no – all that means is no, not now; so ask them when they can help.
- How do we know that strategy will work? What evidence of results have you seen and where have you seen such results? And however good the results are, are they what you are looking for, especially from a standards and sustainability point of view?
- What are the details of the strategy? In particular, it's the small points, the subtleties which make the difference. Key to the strategy of a successful lasagne is making sure that it has had a bit of time to cool before being eaten after being taken from a piping hot oven and before being placed on the table. Small point but it's a difference which makes the difference.

NB's experience

One important learning point is that if so far you have not achieved the change you want, then do consider whether it is that the strategy selected is not an effective one and/or the strategy is not being implemented properly. For example, a very simple basic strategy for creating financial independence is to 'spend less than you earn and save the rest'. Common sense? Yes! Common practice? No!

Ifs & buts
What if I can't find a strategy?
Keep looking! One strategy of people who meet their goals is *persistence*!

What getting a strategy really means
- You will know <u>how</u> to do it.
- You will know where to get brilliant strategies.
- You will know how to discover the nuances that make the difference.

Step 4: Give ATTENTION at TACTICAL level
Get tactical to ensure vision into action

	Attention	Immersion	Momentum
Brain	✔		
Emotion	✔		
Strategy	✔		
Tactics	●		

Concept
But a strategy will not work unless we can decide what we are going to actually do: day-by-day and hour-by-hour. For example, you've decided to become an artist, give up your day job and work on your art during the better part of the day from the point of view of both natural light and your personal energy. And you're working in a restaurant in the evening to pay the rent. But what will you do: how will you get your stuff into galleries? How will you be able to afford those giant canvases?...What's the detail?

We now need detail. If we're making the word's best lasagne, it's not enough to say 'place alternate layers of pasta and meat sauce'. It's not enough to say 'put one layer of pasta and then cover that with approx. similar amount of meat sauce'. No, what we need is:

1. At the bottom of the dish put a 1cm thick layer of meat sauce.
2. Cover that with 0.5 cm depth of béchamel sauce.
3. Cover that with one layer of pasta.

4. Repeat that cycle four times.
5. Cover final level of pasta with just béchamel sauce.
6. Cover that with a hard Italian cheese.

Now that may not seem such a big deal unless you happen to be in the world lasagne-making championships. It's the detail which is crucial: those explicit six points give you a much greater opportunity of success. And you might seek even greater detail on the type of hard Italian cheese, and when you say 'cover', to what depth? Uniformly? As it comes? Detail is crucial because:

■ It gives confidence that you are reproducing the success strategy.
■ It gives confidence that your expert really does know what he/she is talking about.

Example

Tim had several months ago realised the (now) obvious point that to write his book he needed to become a *writer*.
But two subtleties he had only just realised were that:
■ He must write – whatever his mood and in particular even if he didn't feel like doing it.
■ He must not judge the quality of his writing, but write.

For you: reflection and things to do
Tactics are how you begin to deliver on your dream. Do not start out on the journey unless you are sure of as many of details as you can. You're looking here for the formula, the recipe. Get really good at replicating the subtleties. If you are generating sales letters to create new business for your organisation, yes it's important that you *do* those letters but equally it is important that you have the correct *content* in those letters.

NB's experiences
Much advice for realising your dreams can be strong on the big picture, even powerful on the emotional engagement, but the *key is in*

the detail: how *exactly* do you re-design your own garden, now that you believe you can?

And that of course is why I am imploring you to take full note of the subtleties of these points!

Ifs & buts
How do I know if I have got enough detail, if I have got the necessary tactics? When you feel confident that you can follow the steps with a minimum number of errors.

What detailing tactics really means
- You will create brain/time-friendly detail.
- You WILL make it happen: no question of that.
- You will see step-by-step accumulating progress.

Step 5: Create IMMERSION at BRAIN level
Getting resourceful

	Attention	Immersion	Momentum
Brain	✔	●	
Emotion	✔		
Strategy	✔		
Tactics	✔		

Concept
We're back to what happens at Brain level – at logical, personal software level. But this time we are going into immersion phase. The phase at which we become totally 'enveloped' by what is happening. And this is where we ensure our state is one which will guarantee success.

Your *state* will have a profound impact on the progress you make with the change you seek. Will all know that 'how we are' or our state has such an impact. We all know that there are days when we are able to get a lot done. We all know there are days when we feel 'rubbish'. But what we perhaps haven't made fully conscious is how much that state is under our personal management.

Firstly: what kind of state do we need to get personal change to happen? We want to be:

- **Focused,** i.e. to be able firstly to decide what is important and secondly to concentrate on what is important and how to manage that and to avoid distracters and blockers getting in the way.
- **Energetic,** i.e. we need to possess the energy to get done what it is necessary to get done.
- **Light-hearted,** i.e. to be able to not get too stressed nor overly serious about the day-to-day hassles we are likely to face.
- **Inclined to take action,** i.e. able, once having decided what's important, to actually take action: to do it.

And how do we achieve those states?

- **Choice**. We recognise that every day, from the point at which we wake and full consciousness kicks in, we can start making choices about how we want to be, about what kind of person we are and about what kind of results we are seeking. If something is irritating, we don't have to be irritated; simply decide whether that is the best option. When it is raining, we don't have to be gloomy. When our business plan is rejected, we don't have to feel dejected.
- **Personal well-being**. We recognise that our state is a function of both our mental and our physical health. And that our physical and mental health is a function of us taking care of ourselves, from proper nutrition to sufficient sleep.
- **Flip-siding**. We choose specifically to be a possibility thinker: by looking at the possibilities in a situation. We've just been made redundant. Will that hold back our career opportunities? Only if we allow it to do so.

Example

Pierre so wanted to be fit. He got so angry with himself for not exercising. He did a lot of international travel in his job, with a lot of time on planes and a lot of time stuck at airports. As far as he was concerned, that was good working time: to clear his e-mail, follow through on actions. And then he'd have more time when 'down on the ground' for proper exercise. Why wasn't it happening?

Pierre was right in one way. What a fantastic opportunity to clear his work? But what Pierre needed to establish first was getting into the right kind of state for taking action.

For you: reflection and things to do

Before any significant personal change, work on physical and mental health first. And you may well have recognised that, and are keen to work on desire 1 from our list of seven.

No athlete would consider going for the change they are seeking without training, without mental and physical preparation. How will you get the change you are seeking without your mental and physical preparation?

NB's experiences

Certainly for me this has been one of the greatest learning points: that by definition change requires you to wrestle with your conditioned mental processes and your conditioned muscles. So you need to be in the best state possible for as long as possible to get change to happen.

Ifs & buts

I'd like to know more about physical and mental health and flip-siding.
If this is important to you, study desire 1.

What getting resourceful really means

- You will learn how to love change.
- You will learn how to love learning.
- You will learn how to be resourceful.

Step 6: Create IMMERSION at EMOTION level
Using the pain/pleasure lever

Concept

In level 2 of the immersion phase, having addressed the logical side, we now address the complementary side: our emotional side. We recognise that in essence humans take action

	Attention	Immersion	Momentum
Brain	✔	✔	
Emotion	✔	●	
Strategy	✔		
Tactics	✔		

either to increase pleasure or to avoid pain. And therefore to get emotional engagement, to get a connection at both heart and gut level, we will be asking ourselves these powerful questions:

Q1: What will I gain by the change? What's the benefit to me? What's the return on the investment for me?

Q2: Why haven't I changed so far? What pleasure do I get from where I am?

Q3: What pain do I associate with making the change? What's holding me back?

Q4: What will be the cost if I don't make the change? In every sense: financial, emotional, personal, my relationships?

With each of these questions, it is important that we delve beyond our initial superficial response and ask 'and what else?'

As humans, part of our defence mechanism, part of our coping strategy for day-to-day survival is to be good at rationalising, at defending, at finding logic for our continued behaviour. These four questions dig beyond the rationalisation. Putting it bluntly, they will deal with the 'personal bullshit', which can be the biggest blocker to our progress.

Example

Jane was married with two small children. Smoking was her stress management strategy. She knew all the intellectual stuff about it being bad for her health and a poor example for the children. She did want to change, but it hadn't happened so far.

Here's the questioning for Jane:

Q1: What will you gain by giving up smoking?
Better health, better skin. Will personally smell better and be able to smell better. *And what else?* Feeling that I am in control of my actions. The breaking of an addiction. *And what else?* Well, a much better role model for the children. And my husband would be delighted because I know he finds it a right pain. *And what else?* I'd win respect from some of my closest friends who I know think I'm so pathetic for not having kicked the habit. And I hope that when I do I'll have more energy for the other projects I have in mind.

Q2: Why haven't you changed? What pleasure do you get from where you are?
It's great for when I am stressed. It's relaxing in the evenings with a glass of wine. It's social. It stops me putting on weight. *And what else?* To be honest, I know it's crazy but it does feel a little bit sophisticated. And I am fed up of being told what to do by every one. Crikey, it's the one dangerous thing I do in my whole life!

Q3: What pain do you associate with making this change?
It's going to be really hard to let go of smoking. What will I do about stress and relaxation? What will I do about those quiet moments with a cup of coffee and those quick drags to keep me going on the endless round with the toddlers?

Q4: What's the cost if I don't make the change?
Human and monetary. Smoking costs me a lot of money. Not just the direct costs, but also in subtle ways such as needing to get my clothes dry-cleaned more often. On the human side, well there's no history of cancer in our family but then I'm the first serious smoker, so...

Reflection and things to do

To gain acceleration in the change you want, to really push yourself past the tipping point, the point of no return, be very honest with your pain/pleasure questions. Very honest. Scare yourself. Go on!

NB's experiences

Answered with care, these questions are brilliant. I use them regularly when doing one-to-one coaching. They cause profound shifts for individuals. They will get you more focused than you have ever been before on the change you want.

Ifs & buts

How do I know if I am being truly honest with myself when answering these questions?

Being able to ask that question implies you have sufficient self-awareness to ensure that you needn't bullshit yourself. So don't. Your personal integrity will develop throughout the questioning process: it's part of creating personal change.

It's also an area where a good personal buddy can help.

What the pain/pleasure lever really means

- You will experience a powerful lever for change.
- You will gain greater clarity over what stopped you last time.
- You will gain some instant momentum.

Step 7: Create IMMERSION at STRATEGIC level
Break and date

Concept

Our overall strategy in this immersion phase is to break down the change we are trying to make so that it becomes *brain- and time-friendly.* Brain-friendly means that it is attractive to us in that we can see benefits, brain-friendly in that we feel we can actually do it, brain-friendly in

	Attention	Immersion	Momentum
Brain	✔	✔	
Emotion	✔	✔	
Strategy	✔	●	
Tactics	✔		

that we feel it is approachable. By time-friendly we mean that it will fit into a busy schedule.

To make a task brain and time friendly, we work toward the following parameters: we break the task down firstly into small enough chunks that we feel 'yep, I could do that'. Thus:

- Not lose two stone in weight, but lose two pounds per month.
- Not write a book, but write a chapter a fortnight.
- Not find a soul-mate, but be meeting a least a couple of new people per month.

When we have the resulting brain-friendly chunk of work, we then check to see whether it is also time-friendly. A good period of time is 45 minutes. A lot of work can be done in a dedicated 45 minutes. Much less than that and we have little chance of getting to our best thinking. More than that and we may have more difficulty in finding the time.

Once you have broken it down, 'date-stamp' it. Date-stamp it to some time when you feel it will be good to achieve it and then put it into your dairy and/or your wall planner.

Example

Sara's business start-up simply wasn't happening. She was thinking about it. And to a certain extent she was excited about it. But the whole exercise seemed too large, too daunting. So she broke it down. She decided to do it as a series of questions:

- What do I want to achieve through my business?
- How will I get customers?
- What is my pricing policy?
- How will I grow the business?
- What funding support do I need?

And then she broke each of those down, until they were approximately 45-minute chunks of time. And then she date-stamped those, giving them specific dates in November when they would be addressed.

A great tip therefore, to help you with break and date is to ask: Who?, What?, Where?, When? and How?

For you: reflection and things to do
Nothing happens without attention. And attention happens through break and date. Anything you wish to achieve. Break and date. And if it is not attractive yet then you have not broken it down enough.

NB's experiences
This is an important one for those visionaries and big picture individuals out there: get good at break (and break, and break) and date. There comes a point when anything is brain- and time-friendly.

Ifs & buts
How far do I break?
There are two criteria: the job becomes attractive to do and you can do it in time slots of approximately 45 minutes.

What creating immersion really means
- You will experience 'easy' change.
- You will find that change is a 'no-brainer'.
- You will get rapid progress where you've had poor results before.

Step 8: Create TACTICS at IMMERSION level
Commit to plan

	Attention	Immersion	Momentum
Brain	✔	✔	
Emotion	✔	✔	
Strategy	✔	✔	
Tactics	✔	●	

Concept
Things happen when they are visible. How about if every time you sat down in your study area (haven't got one? Now is the time to create one if you are serious about personal change – anywhere will do), there it was staring you in the face? How about if every time you logged onto your PC, your calendar showed your commitments *to yourself*?

These personal commitments are easier to keep if they are 'in yer face', i.e. they are visible.

It must be there as a reminder. Monday 0630: write for 45 minutes. Friday lunch-time, 1230-130: go swimming/do 10 lengths. These are our personal contracts. This is where we manage ourselves. This is not about time management. It's actually about managing ourselves. We're setting up personal commitments.

So, two recommendations:

Firstly, the wall planner. Get a one-year wall planner and mark in important dates and commitments: holiday, birthdays, project deadlines. Then taking a very different coloured pen, indicate your personal deadlines, your personal milestones.

Secondly, transfer all of those dates to your personal diary, and make sure that is always with you. Ensure you don't accept any commitment unless it falls outside your plans.

Example

Tim had decided that his personal wealth project had four stages:

Stage 1 was current situation: he wanted to know exactly what that was by the end of the month.
Stage 2 was getting out of all debt bar the mortgage and his car loan. That was to be done by Christmas.
Stage 3 was to start saving: firstly for his pension. That was to be up and running and part of his normal way of life by spring.
Stage 4 was to have some money to start investing. That was by Christmas in a year's time.

He bought a brilliant wall planner and some coloured felt pens and he got everything onto that planner. He transferred key dates to his personal diary and to his task list. He was now covering every angle.

For you
Once you have completed your break and date, turn those into visible non-forgettable personal commitments by entering them in a highly visible wall planer and then also entering them into your personal diary.

NB's experiences
We do things when we want to *and* they are in our face. The challenge is that we can only hold so much in our foremost consciousness. Ensure what is truly important to you is present in such consciousness through this approach.

Ifs & buts
I'm not a wall planner kind of person.
Perhaps that's a limiting mindset? Try it and see how rapidly your dreams start happening.

What creating tactics really means
- You will not be able to forget what needs to be done.
- You will have an instant TTD (things to do) list.
- You will experience change at the fully 'switched on/in yer face' level.

Step 9: Create MOMENTUM at BRAIN level
Pareto Power

	Attention	Immersion	Momentum
Brain	✔	✔	●
Emotion	✔	✔	
Strategy	✔	✔	
Tactics	✔	✔	

Concept
We're now into our momentum phase; change is happening, but we want to keep it happening. We're indebted to the nineteenth century Italian economist Pareto for highlighting the fact that in many many processes, 80% of the result comes from just 20% of the effort.

Change desired	20%
Healthier	walk OR
	Drink water
Wealthier	Save £10/month

And that is fantastic news for those of us dedicated to serious personal change. To get the change we seek, we must identify what are the most important factors – the 'vital few' factors which will give the most significant change – and then dedicate our attention (see above) to those. In fact most specifically we must not try to do everything because when we do, we often actually achieve nothing.

Example

When Lucy had her health blitz, her magazine-inspired detox, she tended to 'go mad' and try to do everything. And was very frustrated a few days later when typically she felt nothing had been achieved apart from feeling wretched. Lucy changed her approach and decided that she would work on just a few vital areas at any one time. First (month 1), she stopped smoking. Second (month 2), she started taking proper exercise and made that walking because she hated the gym, and then (month 3) worked on her finances by cutting up one credit card a month. Hey, it was working.

For you: reflection and things to do
In any change you want, decide what is the high pay off part, e.g.:
- Health: give up smoking or cut down on binge drinking.
- Money: stop using high interest credit card.

There is always a Pareto factor which you can do. Write the book. Do 1000 words/day. Can't do 1000? Do 100? Can't get to the gym today? Walk around the area in which you work, four times for a brisk 20 minutes.

NB's experiences
This is a delightful factor for causing real breakthrough. It does worry those who like completeness, who feel they like to do things 'properly'. But do remember, when you try to do everything you can so often consequently do nothing.

Ifs & buts

But surely it is important that you do everything eventually, otherwise you have not got the change you seek?

Change is rarely on/off. To a certain extent you are never fully a non-smoker. And much change is a gradual process. Pareto gets that change off to a bang, to a massive 'head-start'.

Then over time the change will be completed.

What taking a Pareto decision really means

- You will gain massive early results.
- You will achieve absolute clear focus.
- You will continue to build momentum.

Step 10: Create MOMENTUM at EMOTION level

Breaking the pattern

	Attention	Immersion	Momentum
Brain	✔	✔	✔
Emotion	✔	✔	●
Strategy	✔	✔	
Tactics	✔	✔	

Concept

The brain is pattern-seeking: it needs to be from an evolutionary point of view. We must be able to recognise things easily and turn them into safe/unsafe decisions and be able to do that rapidly. But the downside of that evolutionary wired-in process is that it is often difficult to break patterns, especially poor habits.

Here we wish to break the pattern that has been established over many, many years probably. It could be that this habit, perhaps procrastination, perhaps looking at the worst case scenario, is something that we've done all our life, or maybe it's a habit we picked up and have just been using the last few years. But it has undoubtedly become a habit and therefore to get the change we require we will need to do a significant breaking of that pattern.

To stop our excess drinking we might catch the bus to work so that we have to catch the bus home and it is simply too difficult to 'stop off' at the pub.

To get ourselves to write each morning we might leave the house 45 minutes earlier, get the quiet earlier train on which we just meditate and mull over a few plot ideas and then when we get into Birmingham, we stop at a coffee shop, buy a latte and write for 45 minutes.

The purpose of all of these is very simply to break the neural and often muscular conditioning that has been set up over time. The good news is that we can set up a new conditioning: a conditioning by which we do write every lunchtime, or 'say no' to desserts in the staff canteen on a week-day or do take up every dinner invitation as we never know who we might meet even though dinner hosts are so tactless about out inability to find the right person...

Example

Here is an assortment of pattern interrupts – simply so that you get the idea:

Wellness/fitness/weight loss
- Do something now, e.g. go for a walk/chuck all rubbish food out of the fridge.
- Give up one unhelpful food for one month. Decide now.
- Find someone who will support you. Decide now.
- Invest some money in a personal trainer. Decide now.
- Read an inspiring book on the subject. Decide now.

Stopping smoking
- Do something now, e.g. crush the current packet.
- Decide not to smoke for just 24 hours and then decide again.
- Buy four different books on people you admire who did smoke and no longer do so. Read them.

Getting the book written
- Do something now: write 500 words. Don't judge. Just write.
- Go on: invest in the lap-top so that you can word-process almost anywhere.

Creating financial independence

■ Do something now: reduce one regular expenditure and initiate it now. E.g. change an insurance premium for a lower one simply by ringing around.

■ Get a jar: put £1 in it at the end of every day. Every month, save what is in the jar.

Developing the career we seek

■ Do a helpful diagnostic, e.g. strength-finder or mbti. Arrange it now.

■ Talk to someone who does the job you fancy doing. Telephone them now.

Creating the relationship you want

■ Do something now: get some time with your partner and just talk.

Being happy

■ Do something now: whatever is happening, decide to be happy.

■ Get rid of one thing from your life which bugs you. Do it now.

One very important pattern interrupt which we will use in several of our strategies is simply not to be overly sympathetic towards the process of non-change. Sometimes we do give someone or ourselves a lot of sympathy for 'it being hard to change'. But there comes a time when the poor behaviour needs to be broken. More on this later.

For you: reflection and things to do

However confident you are of getting the change you seek, always build in as many pattern interrupts you can.

NB's experiences

Long-term conditionings can have been built up over a life-time. That is why pattern interrupt must be carried out. Silly ones can be very effective and you probably use many such as putting on some favourite music and playing it very loud while hoovering. It's simply an extension of that idea.

Ifs & buts
What happens if the pattern interrupt doesn't work?
It wasn't enough of an interrupt or try it again or make it bigger or louder or...

What creating a pattern interrupt really means
- You will finally let go of old habits.
- You will re-wire new habits.
- You will gain rapid momentum.

Step 11: Getting a STRATEGY at MOMENTUM level
Breaking through

	Attention	Immersion	Momentum
Brain	✔	✔	✔
Emotion	✔	✔	✔
Strategy	✔	✔	●
Tactics	✔	✔	

Concept
You're really close now to getting this to be a permanent change. You're well into the momentum part. So now is the time for some real honesty – not that you haven't been honest before. But what still needs to be done? Are there any final blockers that you are concerned about which could stop you being successful? Because you need to explicitly identify them as blockers, so that we can address them. Have there been stumbling blocks in the past? What were they?

Examples

Are these blockers for you?

Wellness/fitness/weight loss
- How stupid do you think you'll feel if you do end up looking great and then relapse within a few months?

Stopping smoking
- You can't see a life as a non-smoker?

Getting the book written
- What your friends might think of the sex scenes in your book?
- What your mum might think of the sex scenes in your book?

Creating financial independence
- You simply have so many commitments on your money already.

Developing the business you want
- What happens if your new start-up goes bust and you end up with significant debt?

Creating the relationship you want
- You're frightened that despite all this you simply won't meet anyone.

Being happy
- Being honest, if you can be happy you'll have nothing to complain about.

For you: reflection and things to do
Here are five very common deep-down definitive blockers which it is worth admitting to and deciding to do something about:

1. **Fear.** Remember the title of Susan Jeffers' book: *Feel the fear and do it anyway*. Manage everything you can and then feel the fear and do it anyway. Fear is a significant part of any change process. It's normal. It's there as a check and think – rightly. It's not there as a stop, necessarily.
2. **What might people might think?** Indeed. Respect their views. Take their wisdom. Then do it anyway.
3. **Uncertainty.** It's a normal part of the change process. You will feel uncertain. Of course. But all of our ideas are there in place to reduce that uncertainty, especially when we create our Vivid, Explicit, Mental Model.
4. **Not enough time.** There rarely is. That's one of the excitements of being a creative person with lots of possibilities in his/her life. Work smart. Use the ideas we are reviewing.
5. **Where on earth do I start?** Read on.

NB's experiences

Spot the blockers and simply don't accept them.
List them, address them. Delight in beating them.

Ifs & buts

Some blockers are so hard. Some seem impossible.
They will be hard: work at them slowly and surely. Many seem
impossible, but when you look back in a few months' time you will be
amazed at how much you have done.

What overcoming blockers really means

- You will finally overcome old-established blockers.
- You will gain rapid momentum.
- You will disconnect from non-resourceful states.

Step 12: Bold first steps

Take it away!

	Attention	Immersion	Momentum
Brain	✔	✔	✔
Emotion	✔	✔	✔
Strategy	✔	✔	✔
Tactics	✔	✔	●

Concept

You're there. Now is the time to start turning
unsteady steps into bold steps, to turn up the
speed from walking to jogging. With
momentum it becomes much much harder to stop us.

Example

Tim had reams and reams of jottings and plans concerning his new
start-up. His bold step was to go and find his office and go to the
agency for his first temporary assistant.

For you: reflection and things to do

For every change you want, attach a big bold step. Be audacious.

NB's experiences

When stuck, take a step. Make a phone-call. Use a book for an idea. And
then another one. Before you know where you are it is a part of your life.

Ifs & buts

I really don't have any left!
Good, because this is where we work on the specifics which you want.

What taking a bold first step really means

- You will absolutely definitely be committing to change.
- You will start seeing results.
- You're completing your personal contract with yourself.

Seven applications for our new-found skills: achieving seven desires

You're ready now. You've done all the ground-work. You understand the three overall phases of personal change, AIM: Attention, Immersion and Momentum. And you realise that for each phase to work we need to address four levels. We need to get change at Brain level, at Emotion level, at Strategic level and at Tactical level, i.e. 12 overall steps. We'll *AIM 4 BEST* – just as expressed by Michelangelo.

We could leave it there: you now have an excellent detailed *generic* understanding of what to do. But we're not going to, we're now going to apply those ideas to the seven most frequently expressed desires. I want you to be absolutely confident that you can achieve your desires.

They are of course:
- Desire 1: To lose weight, get fit, feel well and attractive.
- Desire 2: To give up smoking.
- Desire 3: To write and publish a book.
- Desire 4: To achieve financial independence.
- Desire 5: To establish the career you want and/or the business of your dreams.
- Desire 6: To find and keep true love.
- Desire 7: To be happy.

Go to the one(s) you want help with and/or read a couple to help with the changes you are seeking in your life.

Chapter 4
The applications:
achieving seven desires

Desire 1: To lose weight, get fit, feel well and attractive
Desire 2: To give up smoking
Desire 3: To write and publish a book
Desire 4: To achieve financial independence
Desire 5: To establish the career you want and/or the business of your
            dreams
Desire 6: To find and keep true love
Desire 7: To be happy

Desire 1: To lose weight, get fit, feel well and attractive

We've chosen this desire to work on first. It is one of the most fundamental of human desires: who doesn't want to feel good and look good? We are also considering this desire because it is often forgotten that genuine health and wellness is the number one factor for enabling personal change. Wellness, both mental and physical, gives us the inclination to act. In fact more fundamentally it could be said that when personal change is easy for us we are at our peak of wellness.

So, what is the desire as it is commonly expressed? Perhaps one of these:

To be fit
To lose some weight
To get back into a size 10/12/14
To be well
To feel well
To feel attractive again
To stop feeling and looking 15 years older than I really am
To have energy
To start doing something in the evening
To be able to play kick-about in the park with the kids.

We are going to use the 12 steps, which you now know so well: three phases (AIM), four levels (BEST) to get the change you seek. Along the way we are going to need to find out exactly what you want, the interdependencies between weight loss, the psychology of personal change and attractiveness.

Step 1: Give ATTENTION at BRAIN level

Adjusting your mindset to support your change
Our fundamental premise: mindset drives action. Action drives results. So for powerful change, ensure the mindset is supportive.

To make progress we must address our mindset. Many people have developed very limiting mindsets about their capabilities in this area. For example:

> " I will never lose any weight"
> "I'm going to be stuck with this asthma for the rest of my life"
> "My gym training scheme is only ever short-term"

Here are some suggested mindset statements, particular to this desire:

- **I understand why I want this.** Well do you? Why are you doing it? There are two good reasons and one very poor reason. The first good reason is for your health, well-being and longevity. The second reason is for your attractiveness, how you feel about yourself and the consequent impact on your self-esteem. The one bad reason is because of social conditioning, e.g. that you feel you must be this weight or be able to wear these clothes or have a certain body shape. Because you will never be able to meet all of the conditions that society's fantasies expect of you. That's why we only see these people in films and colour magazines. Decide that you will understand why you want this and it will be for one or both of the two good reasons.
- **I regularly remind myself what true attractiveness is.** Because real attractiveness is about the ability to laugh, smile, 'be sexy' (very different to 'looking' sexy). So what if you're a little plump? Hey, not everyone wants to go out with a garden rake? But, you say, men like big breasts, women like small butts. No, these are generalisations. And anyway that's just part of the relationship, the body chemistry part. A very important part of course. A hugely fun part, true. But it is not the whole story. And if you decide not to make it so, your attractiveness need depend only in part on your physical desirability: it can be much more about who and what you are rather than how you look.

- **I decide that I want to be well, attractive and sexy, but in my sphere of reference.** Decide what is attractive for you. What is sexy for you? What kind of style will allow your attractiveness to shine through?
- **I can. I can definitely achieve this through the correct approach.** You can. It's the mindset which will make the differences you are already seeing. Too much work in this area simply plays to the general social conditioning. You're not going to do that.
- **I can be proud of my body.** It's been neglected. I've been living 'outside of it', expecting it to look after itself. I'm going to live inside it again and look after it.
- **I accept the aging process.** Because by trying to reverse it, by attempting to look 22 when I'm actually 43 is not kidding any one. And it's just causing me more frustration.
- **When I am jealous of youth, I stop and think.** What am I jealous of? Freedom, sex, fun? Because each of these are available to me now should I choose them.
- **I appreciate the wisdom that I am gaining** – day in day out I'm getting smarter. I won't allow others to encourage me to behave in a stupid manner.
- **I can restore my health.** The body has one of the world's greatest pharmacological factories. I can break the connection with quick fix and allow my body to heal and overcome any challenges I am currently facing, And I will allow time for that to happen.
- **I can become the world's leading expert on my medical condition and assist the healing process.** No one is as interested in your challenge as you: become the expert.
- **I understand that attractiveness is not just a physical thing: I enjoy being mentally attractive.** I will keep reading, keep learning. And stay fascinating.
- **I can break the link between food and reward/compensation.** When things are going well, when things are going badly, I can break the need immediately to turn to food and/or drink.

Keep the ones which help in your note book. Add your own and notes from people you meet and admire.

Step 2: Give ATTENTION at EMOTION level

Getting passionate and creating a vivid, explicit mental model
Our fundamental premise: we must get engagement at heart and gut level as well as at brain and intellectual level. Here we create a vivid, explicit mental model.

This is critical: getting the right 'picture' of what you want. Often the image we currently hold is of someone 'projected' by the media. And this applies to both men and women. What is a natural evolution for your body? Think forward a couple of years. Attributes such as sexiness are not dependent solely upon looks. This is where you need to do some serious work. You need pen and paper or screen and keyboard. Here are the questions: to each you must respond rapidly and with honesty.

Within our framework of weight loss, fitness, wellness and attractiveness, what do you want? Answer in full in a sentence or two, but ensure it is a want, not a don't want. Don't write down, 'I don't want to look fat any more'. What do you *want*?

I want to be able to wear anything and feel good in my clothes.

And is there anything else?

I want to be a size 10 again. I want to feel healthy and fit. I want more energy.

Ok, whatever it is you want, imagine you are now there. No if or buts, you are there: what are you seeing? No superficial responses such as 'the new slim me' or 'me, but with more muscles'. That kind of thinking is why you haven't got the change you really wanted in the past! Engage fully; what do you really see? Specifically, now.

Confident happy ~~pear~~ person.

Looking good in my clothes and feeling sexy.

Happy & healthy with vitality and taste for life.

Not wheezing or feeling bloated

And what else do you see? feeling fit & healthy.

A partner who supports me and thinks I am sexy.

And what do you feel?

Really good about myself and healthy.

10 years younger!!!

And what do you hear?

Comments on how good I look.

The words I 'love you'!

Now write again – *what do you want?* But this time, write around 500 words of sensory rich description. And if you need help, try these:

- What do you mean by fit? ~~Being~~ Able to go to me gym and enjoy it!
- What do you mean by well?
- Where will you shop for your clothes?
- Where will you run? a size 10 rail!!
- How far will you run? park & cunony)
  10 miles

You'll have your own description, but perhaps it'll be something like this:

> In 12 months' time I am going to be exactly 2kg lighter, I am very toned so I appear even lighter. I am keeping my body shape; I like being quite curvy and men tell me that's something they find attractive about me. I am working at walking a lot more in whatever the weather, I have dropped a lot of my pathetic avoidance of rain and the cold and that has helped my complexion which to be honest was becoming overly laden with synthetic chemicals. I am doing a course in the evening as well as meeting new people. I think I am becoming more interesting: I feel more attractive.

OR

> By this time next year I will have got rid of my 'beer belly'. I realise I have simply been trying to get rid of it too fast. A 'smarter' routine at the gym and simply stopping going to the pub every lunch-time will make the difference. I'm also going to sort out my wardrobe, my clothes and get fewer decent ones; I know I'll look a lot more attractive once I have done that. And finally and pretty radically for me I am going to get my hair sorted out: the fact is I am receding rapidly. But what the heck, I'm going to stop trying to hide it.

Step 3: Give ATTENTION at STRATEGIC level

Selecting strategies to guarantee success
We need strategies for losing weight/getting fit/feeling well/attractiveness.

Whatever strategy we select it needs to accommodate the following:
- The strategy must not be dependent solely upon genetic advantage. Imagine for example some cosmetics products which are advertised by supermodels. The advertisement implies that because of the cosmetics product the supermodel is particularly attractive. In fact it is pretty well the reverse of that. Because the supermodel is attractive, the cosmetic product is selling well.
- The strategy must be a holistic one, i.e. it must not create one benefit e.g. weight loss while at the same time doing harm to our wellness elsewhere.
- It must recognise that wellness is a different term to fitness. Deliberately so. We will be focusing on wellness.
- Weight loss needs to be understood for what it is. Why do you wish to lose weight? Because you are actually overweight or because you wish to look like a certain model?
- Wellness and weight loss must go hand in hand otherwise neither are sustainable.

Specifically on wellness:
- Wellness will be specific to your body type, your body shape. A key component will be becoming more sensitive to your body and its requirements. It is an individual strategy you are seeking.
- Wellness requires a mind-body approach, e.g. it is very difficult to feel well if we are having say financial concerns.
- Wellness cannot be fixed by just one aspect, e.g. food, without say addressing sleep. All aspects of our life are absolutely and intimately interconnected with our wellness.

Specifically on weight loss:
- Weight loss must be linked to a sustainable strategy.
- Weight loss must be linked to the psychology of the process.

Specifically on attractiveness:

- It is you who will make you attractive. What is attractive?
- Someone who looks their best, for *them.*
- Someone who is both interested and interesting.
- Someone who dresses well for their body shape and personal colouring.

Specifically on fitness:

- We seek fitness for overall health, feeling good and attractiveness.
- Achieving fitness does not need to be unpleasant.

In order to meet the above we have four sustainable strategies:
Strategy 1 *Wellness = M-E-D-S*
Strategy 2 *Perfect weight = T-E-F-L*
Strategy 3 *Attractiveness = Authenticity + Golden rule*
Strategy 4 *Fitness = CV & Resistance*

Each strategy is self-contained, and can be used and selected independently of the others. But each strategy also supports the others and over time you may well wish to adopt all of them.

Strategy 1 Wellness = M-E-D-S
Our first strategy, our foundation strategy, is our strategy for wellness.
This we will summarise as MEDS. MEDS is a four-part, holistic
programme for returning to great health.

MEDS is our abbreviation for meditation, exercise, diet and sleep. All
four components are essential to you getting the wellness and
ultimately any physical change including weight loss which you desire.
Your strategy may well have failed in the past possibly because it has
been too quick fix and probably because it has not treated the body as
a whole. Here's MEDS:

Meditation
We'll ensure you know how to take time out to relax. When there is
undue stress in the body it easily adopts addictive tendencies: to the
wrong foods for example! When there is stress in the body it is not as

keen to take exercise. We'll encourage you to find a form of meditation which works well for you.

Exercise
This is essential not only for the well-being of the body but also of course an exercised body has an inclination to act (compare that with a 'couch potato': he/she can just about 'zap' the TV channels).

Diet
We'll be looking at appropriate fuels for energy, getting balance across food types. Nothing odd, weird or unbalanced. Again this is where many strategies fall apart. You need energy for change and appropriate selection of foods for wellness.

Sleep
If you are suffering from sleep debt because of insufficient sleep or poor quality sleep then you'll find change close to impossible. We'll ensure you get full, quality sleep. Without proper sleep, your body will be struggling to return you to full wellness.

You'll get what you want in mind/body with MEDS. The breakthrough will come with a strategy which works. We'll go into detail on each of the elements of MEDS and how to get it to work for you, in Step 4, Tactics, coming up soon. Go straight there if it's the only strategy you wish to work on.

Strategy 2 Perfect weight = T-E-F-L
What is our strategy for achieving our perfect weight? Once again, it is in four parts: give easy attention to each of the four components.
T is *type* of body; your body shape. E is amount you *eat*; portion control. F is *food* value. L is *life* psychology.

T: TYPE of body; your body shape
At home, find a quiet 20 minutes. Find a full-length mirror. Take your clothes off. And in the nude, study your body. So, what's up with it? Your view, now. Not some ridiculous colour-supplement view. What would you like to change? You know you can't get a figure like that

model and you wouldn't want to anyway. You know you can't get a chest with muscles like that without supplements. What do you want to change, if anything? Maybe it's losing a little bit of weight, maybe it's some toning of the upper body. Maybe it's your posture. Maybe it's building a bit of muscle.

E: amount you EAT; portion control
If you need to lose weight, eat less. Isn't that obvious? It should be. But we've become a super-size culture: more is apparently better. In fact, as with so many things less is more. Start reducing your portion size. From when you're in the coffee shop (switch from large to medium for 10 days then medium to standard) to at home when you are having supper with the kids.

F: food value
Decide now that you will look at food in an additional way, thinking what value is this giving me? Bear in mind that:

■ You *do* need to eat fruit and vegetables. They are essential for vitamins and minerals. And as is usually the case, it is better to have the real thing rather than vitamin tablets.
■ You will need some protein: there are a vast range of sources, including meat, fish, nut, milk, soya.
■ You will need some complex carbohydrates (e.g. pasta, rice) for long-term energy source.
■ And of course, oxygen (plenty of stretch breaks) and water.

But you do not need:
■ sugar
■ cakes
■ biscuits
■ fizzy drinks!

Broadly speaking, all of these have zero food value.

But finally realise that eating for wellness does not mean lentils and rice all the time. You could eat a burger. But whose burger? Perhaps one you have made yourself so that you know the meat source and there is no rubbish added to the meat. And perhaps don't eat them for lunch and supper every day. This isn't seeming so bad, is it?

L: life psychology
Our choice of what to eat and when to eat is of course not just dictated by our hunger nor by our meal-times. It is also strongly driven by our state: how we are feeling, what has been happening during the day and what is happening in our life.

Thus:
- Feeling fed-up: you might eat more chocolate
- Feeling depressed: you might hit the wine
- Ravenously hungry: you might eat two bowls of cereal in quick succession and then have supper
- Elated: you might celebrate with an extra portion of cake. And then another one.

These are all dangerous habits and can wreck any clear logical weight loss plan we might have. And that is why it is so important of course to work on your state. *When you are in great state, you will not over-eat.* Poor states cause two difficulties: we try to remedy the poor state through some food compensation and then because it was a powerful state, we associate it with food/drink. How do we achieve great state? Start with MEDS. And link it with the work below. And do not forget the fundamental mindset 'I can break the link between reward/compensation and food'.

Details coming up soon in Tactics. Go there now, if you wish.

Strategy 3 Attractiveness = Authenticity + Golden rule

So you want to be attractive? Stop trying to be someone else! You will be most attractive when you are the *best* version of yourself. You are unique, even if you are an identical twin. But you'll soon lose that if you try to be someone else. That doesn't mean you can't learn some great behaviours from others to help you, but work on being the best version of the exciting, unique, one-off you.

Couple that with 'going out' to people. In your own way of course. Often known as the 'golden rule'.

So, to be attractive:

■ Be the best version of you that you can be.
■ Follow the golden rule: give out and you will get back.

Details coming up soon in Tactics. Go there now, if you wish.

Strategy 4 Fitness = CV + Resistance
To be fit, you must invest in your cardio-vascular ability and your resistance work. You knew that already, didn't you? What you want is the tactical level. Coming soon.

Step 4: Give ATTENTION at TACTICAL level

Getting tactical to ensure vision into action
We have our four strategies; how do we make each happen?

We break them into tactics, as follows:

Strategy 1: MEDS
Meditation
Every day spend 10 minutes in the morning and 10 minutes in the evening doing a simple breathing meditation. To do this, simply sit quietly with your eyes closed and follow the flow of your breathing. It is as simple as that. Do not 'try' to do anything special with your breathing, simple be more aware of it. Equally, do not 'try' to get rid of thoughts. Just do it!

Exercise
Every day ensure you walk as much as you can and take the stairs wherever possible. In addition, build into your week as soon as you feel ready three sessions of additional cardio-vascular activity such as jogging, swimming, cycling. Be creative: remember that there are often ways to build in CV/resistance work to the day quite naturally,

through cleaning or playing with the kids or walking back from shopping.

Diet
Chose your food for health. Ensure that you maximise fruit, vegetables, long-term sources of energy (complex carbohydrates) and suitable protein sources. Go for variety. Minimise junk food (food which is highly processed) and zero value food (simple sugars, fizzy drinks, etc.).

Sleep
Each day, wake naturally and feeling refreshed by getting enough quality sleep. Ensure that you 'wind down' easily and sensibly the previous evening. Do not work on the computer or watch TV late into the night.

Strategy 2: Perfect weight

Body type
Think about your body type. How would you describe it? Being sensible, what size management is open to you?

Portion control
Decide:

- When eating out, assuming there is a choice, have the small version. If there is no choice, ask for a smaller portion. No you probably won't get a price reduction, but it's your health we are talking about here.
- When eating at home, eat from a smaller plate, leave space on the plate and do not pile food greater than one layer.
- Eat more slowly and savour food.
- Eat regularly, eat more calories towards the beginning of the day when you need them most.
- Give eating your full attention: don't eat in front of the TV, for example.

Food value
Only eat food with value. Keep non-value foods only as an infrequent treat.

Food psychology

Notice the emotions which encourage you to want certain foods and drinks. Discover other ways to change that emotion and ways to avoid that emotion initially. In particular:

■ Ensure that you are enjoying your food.
■ Do break the myth that all great tasting food is bad for you.
■ Don't become precious about your rituals. It's OK once in a while to break your guidelines.

Strategy 3: Authenticity

Be yourself. Don't let anyone control you or cage you. Be self-referenced and certainly don't be conditioned by society's messages about how you should look. Remember:

■ You are unique.
■ You are attractive in your own way.
■ Think for yourself.
■ Question assumptions and messaging especially about your body and what makes you 'worthwhile'.

Practise using the golden rule: what you tend to give out you'll tend to get back.

■ Be courteous.
■ Thank people, especially in the working environment even if it is their job.
■ Make eye contact.
■ Don't just do the golden rule with special people; do it everywhere.

Strategy 4: Fitness

Here is the ascending scale; start at the beginning and work your way up:

1. Walk as much you can each day.
2. Ensure you walk briskly every day.
3. Take the stairs at every opportunity.
4. Learn how to stretch and keep flexible.
5. Do some jogging.
6. Do some swimming.
7. Do some cycling.

8. Do some gentle weights work.
9. Get specific advice from a personal trainer on how to reach your personal fitness goals.
10. Moderate your plan according to your job.

Aim to be at level 4 over six months and level 8 within 24 months.

Step 5: Create IMMERSION at BRAIN level

Getting resourceful

Our fundamental premise. Although many do give 'attention' to the change they seek, most then move on before the change is completed. We don't fall into that trap. We ensure we immerse ourselves in the change so that the change becomes irreversible.

We should at this stage have a strong inclination to act as we have already (1) created an empowered mindset to support us in this work (2) created a vivid and explicit mental model of what we are seeking (3) identified a strategy which will give us success (4) highlighted the tactics which are necessary to ensure the change happens.

We now reinforce that by shifting from our attention stage to immersion stage and doing our utmost to ensure we have an 'inclination to act' mindset.

We do this by:
- Looking after ourselves:
    - taking time out,
    - getting sleep and
    - getting data deprivation time.
- By using the following affirmations:
    - I am > addictions
    - I am > laziness
    - I am > 'smart-alec' comments of my friends.

Step 6: Create IMMERSION at EMOTION level

Using the pain/pleasure lever

Once again, time for you to do some serious work. We're stepping on the accelerator now. You want this change. Let's get it as quickly as we can.

You need pen and paper or keyboard and screen. Here are your questions:

Q1: What will you gain by the change? Write quickly and without stopping. What is it that you will gain? What attracts you about losing weight/becoming well/more attractive/especially fit?

....

....

....

....

Come on, there's more than that. You won't just look good and feel good. You will feel tremendous. Hey, it's not just that you'll have more energy, you'll actually be able to kick a ball around the park with your children/grand-children. What else will you gain by this change?

....

....

....

....

Q2: Why haven't you changed so far? What pleasure do you get from where you are?

....

....

....

....

No – more honesty needed! If you don't change, there's no chance of ridicule if you fail, is there? Or if you start this, there being comments such as 'oh! another January, another diet, eh'?

....

....

....

....

Q3: What pain do you associate with making the change?

....

....

....

....

That's true, but what about maintaining it for ever more, not just for the summer when you are in a swim suit? Never ever eating another cream bun? Does that worry you?

....

....

....

....

Q4: What will be the cost if you don't make the change? You need to get very explicit on this one.

....

....

....

....

What exactly? What will happen to your health? To your feelings about yourself. It's not so good, is it?

....

....

....

....

Step 7: Create IMMERSION at STRATEGIC level

Break and date

Now review your strategy. Review your pain/pleasure responses. Break your plans down into small, measurable actions. Actions which are brain- and time-friendly. And make them time and date specific. You'll decide yours.

Here are some example ones just so that you have some illustrations for the process:

Tim's actions

On gaining wellness
- Meditate on the train every morning 7.15-7.30.
- On Saturday and Sunday, meditate 9-9.20 and in the late afternoon assuming not out.
- Every work-day lunch-time, walk to the sandwich shop. Buy fruit instead of chocolate (have chocolate bar at the week-end).
- At week-end, take the kids on a 1h bicycle ride, weather permitting.
- Start using alarm as back-up not a primary method of waking.
- Clear all junk out of bedroom so that it's back to relaxing/sleeping and love-making.
- Spend this quarter's bonus on big screen TV for spare room, our 'home cinema'. Get rid of all other TVs around the house.

Sally's actions

On losing weight

- Messages on fridge, on my note book, on my mobile:
    - Eat less
    - Eat value
- Write shopping list every time and never shop when hungry.
- Lose 14lb this year, at a rate of 1 lb/month approx.
- Each morning do 10, increasing to 30, sit-ups, to match and tone to tummy weight loss.
- Ignore everyone else's diet advice. In fact don't really mention it nor make a big deal of it.

Jim's actions

On fitness

- Review finances and find money to join gym and pay for four initial personal trainer sessions. That's a big commitment, but I can do it and I waste money all over the place at the moment, most of it actually un-doing my health!
- Get trainer to show me equipment and get me over tough start-up month and design an initial programme for me.
- Focus on this and get it right. Leave the house extension till this time next year.

Tina's actions

On attractiveness

- Work on toning: buy some dumbbells and do that every morning and evening at home while listening to some good up-beat music.
- Get a good book to guide me on clothes and colours for my body shape and skin tone. Ask for a present from my Mum next birthday to get a session with a consultant if I can find a good one.
- Make an effort with others. Change mindset from 'looking good is enough'. Think more about using my brain.

Right, done yours yet? Come on then! Start writing. Break and date.

Step 8: Create TACTICS at IMMERSION level

Commit to plan

Now that you've got your list of actions, get them onto your wall planner: up on the wall and in every diary you use. Make it clear and bold. In particular ensure you schedule real time, i.e. meditate 7-7.30 not just meditate 7.

Here are some tips:
- Ensure the planner is visible, not hidden in the back bedroom.
- Ensure you have both a big bold visible version and a portable one.
- Mark it with clear graphics and pictures.
- Importantly: celebrate successes with big ticks or smileys; whatever is your style.
- If you are in a buddy set-up: have rewards and celebrations but not counter to the hard work you are doing. E.g. don't celebrate weight loss with a cream bun! Hey, it seems silly, but it happens!
- If at all possible – and it works well for weight loss, days achieved with a good night's sleep, etc. – create a progress chart, too.

Step 9: Create MOMENTUM at BRAIN level

Pareto power

Let's keep our progress moving. Let's keep the immersion going. In every area there are high pay-offs we can create. Once again, here are some examples:

Wellness
- *Decide* to become well. A clear decision and personal contract with yourself is probably the most valuable thing you can do.
- Take time out: slow down; meditate. Start investing in yourself. We are surrounded by machines, but you are not one! Remember that your body works in a very different way.
- Take a break and walk every day.
- Switch simple sugars for fruit. Instead of confectionary, eat a piece of fruit.

Getting fit
- *Decide* to become fit.
- Walk everywhere you can. We drive too much. Become a walker.
- Take the stairs everywhere you can. Unless you really need to, e.g. carrying a heavy case, stop taking the lift. Walk on escalators, too.
- Invest a significant sum for you with the best personal trainer you can find who is in your area and who will help you get into immersion phase.

Losing weight
- *Decide* to lose weight.
- Reduce portion size by 25% for week 1, then 33% week 2, then 50% week 3. Your hunger level will need to adjust. If you still feel ravenously hungry, do a calorie count and check that you haven't gone too far. The recommended daily amounts are: 2000 calories per day female, 2500 per day male.

Becoming attractive
- *Decide* to improve your attractiveness, but think mental as well as physical. With physical there's only so much change you can make unless you're thinking surgery (and why on earth would you want to do that?). But with mental, it is simply a decision to be more attractive.
- Be interesting.
- Be interested.
- Invest a significant sum for you with the best make-over consultant you can find who is in your area to advise on colours/style and (if appropriate) make-up.

Step 10: Create MOMENTUM at EMOTION level

Breaking the pattern
Here are some pattern interrupts to inspire you and give you some ideas:

Wellness

■ Stop on the way home to meditate; you thought you couldn't get the time or space. You can. Pull up somewhere safe and meditate for 10 minutes.

■ Decide to have no sugar for one week, push though the addiction. Notice how much better you feel. You thought you couldn't do it. You can.

■ Make it no alcohol Monday to Thursday. Yes, you can. And you'll feel great for it and you'll appreciate your wine again when you start at the week-end.

Getting fit

■ Travel by public transport; walk the connections.

■ Buy a skipping rope and persevere: it'll improve your co-ordination, too.

Losing weight

■ Create a fixed, reduced list for shopping. Don't allow yourself to shop without it.

■ Shop for food by internet. Restrict what you buy and the saved time can be used for simple toning exercises.

Becoming more attractive

■ Stop reading those trashy magazines and watching those TV programmes which irritate you so much.

■ Get some decent friends. Go out with them. Don't talk work, don't talk TV. Talk life.

Step 11: Getting a STRATEGY at MOMENTUM level

Breaking through

Let's take a look at the blockers you might face and let's handle them:

I simply don't have time.
Accept that. It's a given. As a busy interesting, creative person of course you don't have time *for everything*. And that's your challenge. You're trying to do everything. Decide your priorities. And how can one of those not be your health, your fitness, your wellness and how you feel about yourself: your attractiveness? No, it can't not be. It has to be. Make it so!

People will think I'm weird if I meditate
A surprisingly large number of people do meditate and most of them are very normal! Many in business keep it as their secret weapon. With stuff such as this, stay self-referenced, i.e. do what you feel is important and don't be swayed by the views of others.

I'm caught in a vicious circle; I don't have the energy to go out and get fit
Start small. Start gently. Walk a bit. Swim a bit. And your energy will kick in. The body is designed to be used.

I'd love to lose weight but... I have a family to feed
Great time to introduce them to some excellent practices. Home made chips (baked in the oven while you're helping with homework or whatever) are great, as are homemade burgers (mince, onions, garlic, tomato purée, worcestershire sauce; mix well; shape into patties; grill; serve with salad in sesame baps).

I have a full time job and the canteen is full of dreadful food
There will be something decent in that canteen. And if there isn't, time to start a campaign because others will want something decent, too.

I'd love to be seen as more attractive... I have a fundamental problem: I'm too tall/I have the wrong hair colour

Hey, we all have a fundamental problem; it's known as being human. And if we are the perfect model, the perfect 'flavour of the month', we have another problem and that is it's going to change soon. Be the best version of you that you can. Now.

Step 12: Bold first steps

Take it away!

Here are some suggested big bold first steps:

- Pick up the phone and book someone who will help: a dedicated friend or a specialist such as a personal trainer.
- Pick an area which particularly interests/inspires you, e.g. meditation/yoga. Become an expert on it (but don't delay doing it!).
- Buy a new notebook. Write in it the 12 steps, one per page. Fill each in from memory. You'll be surprised at how well you know them and how much more confident you feel about getting change to happen.
- Go out now, get the wall planner and start filling it in.
- Write your affirmations (e.g. I am greater than this pathetic wish to stay in and watch TV) and stick them around the house.
- Have that conversation with your spouse: explain that you'd like their support (even if they themselves are not interested).
- Chose some actions from the things to do list. Do them.

Things to do

Step 1: Choose brilliant, supporting mindsets. What are the critical ones for you with this desire? That attractiveness is being the best you can be, NOT trying to copy someone else? That you can start eating less? Decide now.

Step 2: Create the most powerful VEMM ever. 'Turn up' the one you created earlier: make it even more vivid. What will you be looking like? How will you be feeling?

Step 3: What's the strategy you MUST give most focus to? Is it M-E-D-S or T-E-F-L or more simply Authenticity + Golden Rule or CV + Resistance.

Step 4: What are the critical tactics you need to employ?

Step 5: Are you inclined to act? Get so you are. NOW.

Step 6: Have you worked your pain/pleasure lever? Are you clear on what's going to happen if this change doesn't happen? What scares you? No, it's good to be scared: it's a reminder of why this is important to you.

Step 7: Have you broken it down, and broken it down. And dated it? DO IT NOW.

Step 8: Is it 'in yer face'?

Step 9: What's the highest payoff you can create in the next 24 hours to get this going?

Step 10: What could stop you? It's only you, you know! Do you truly understand that?

Step 11: Take those first steps, now!

NB's thoughts

This was a number 1 desire for me: getting fit and well again. Ending up in hospital with Guillaine-Barré syndrome and the possibility of being paralysed for life, maybe dying, got me really focused on how to develop excellent wellness and health and fitness. Not surprising really!

If you are in great health, use these ideas to keep that great health. If you are not, whether it's major or minor, be confident you can improve your personal situation, through these simple approaches.

Desire 2: To give up smoking

Desire 2 is to give up smoking. This is an excellent desire to seek. Not simply for the obvious personal benefits, but also from the point of view of becoming an excellent change agent. How come? Because to give up smoking you have to not only deal with more than the logic of *why* you smoke, you need to be able to manage a very complex range of *emotional hooks* which keep you smoking.

So what do you want? Start getting clear and explicit now.

- *To give up smoking – for ever.* That's important. Ad-hoc strategies have a reasonable amount of success in the short term. But we want to create a long-term change.
- *To still be able to enjoy life.* Vital. If as a non-smoker, life is miserable there is something wrong.
- *To not have side effects such as putting on weight, getting stressed, as a result of our quitting.* One reason many return to smoking having been successful initially is because of problems with negative side effects, particularly weight gain and losing a stress management strategy.

Step 1: Give ATTENTION at BRAIN level

Adjusting your mindset to support your change
Premise: mindset drives action. Action drives results. So for powerful change, ensure your mindset is supportive.

Here are some suggested mind-set statements:
- *I can give up smoking and for ever.* People do it all the time. Yes, people do. That doesn't mean it's easy, but people do give it up and they never take it up again. You'll be able to do that. *Drop the one about you can't do it or it won't last.*
- *I am going to make this the last time I give up smoking: I am going to give this as much attention as is necessary to make it happen.* What a great mind-set to have! That this is going to be the last time that this will happen.

And what a fantastic simple strategy, simply over-load the attention until the addiction crumbles. You know this is totally reasonable and guaranteed to work. *Drop the one about you haven't got time to think about giving up smoking.*

- *I recognise that the reason I smoke is complicated. It's a chemical addiction plus many other factors. I will isolate every single factor and break all of them.* Hey, cool! Hunt down every element of addiction and break each element, one by one. You're smart and you know you can do this. *Drop the one about 'I'm simply addicted'. There is no simple here.*
- *I recognise that every day I smoke I am being conned: by me and by the marketeers.* It's true but if it makes you angry, that's excellent. Decide not to be manipulated and 'marketed to' by the image-makers. And don't be conned by yourself; you are worth more than this addiction. You are greater than this addiction. *Drop the one about 'they made me; they got me addicted'. Whatever, now you are in control.*
- *Above all, in smoking I am no longer going to be sympathetic to the challenges I face. I recognise that I am currently acting stupidly.* Hard, isn't it? How about this mindset combined with a pattern interrupt. But you are intelligent. You are. So why are you smoking? Absolutely. *Drop the one about 'it's just too hard'.*

Step 2: Give ATTENTION at EMOTION level

Getting passionate and creating a vivid, explicit, mental model
Premise: we must get engagement at heart and gut level as well as at brain and intellectual level. Here you create your vivid, explicit, mental model.

So, what do you want? Go on, write it down now. Remember to write this statement in a positive 'moving towards' sense. Get plenty of positive statements in there. Not just 'I want give up smoking', but 'I want to become a healthy person and smoking is not a part of that'. 'I want to become a non-smoker'. 'I want to become an ex-smoker'.

THE APPLICATIONS: ACHIEVING SEVEN DESIRES | **89**

Write now, quickly and with energy. What is it you want?

....

....

....

....

What other detail could you add? Excellent. Write.

....

....

....

....

And now imagine that you are there. You've got it.

What do you see?

....

....

....

....

And what else? A bit more money in your pocket? Fewer trips to the
dry cleaners? A whole new range of friends? Cleaner teeth? What else?

What do you hear?

....

....

....

....

Some enthusiastic comments? Often people are not necessarily positive about changes you might make; often based on simple jealousy, of course. But smoking is usually very different: people are normally very enthusiastic. This is cool. People are saying such positive things about how well you have done.

What do you feel?

....

....

....

....

And what else? Of course you feel good. But really good. And being honest, a bit rough at times because of the withdrawal symptoms.

And two bonus sensory-rich questions now that you are an ex-smoker: what do you taste?

....

....

....

....

Food, of course. Drinks of course. You'd forgotten how amazing real organic apple juice was. It's gorgeous.

And what do you smell?

....

....

....

....

It's fantastic. The range of smell you rediscover. The intimate fragrances of your lover. Flowers, again. The original spices as you create your curry from scratch because your love of cooking has returned.

Now pull it all together so that you have around 500 words of sensory-rich description detailing exactly your new life. It'll obviously be your description, but maybe it'll be something like this:

> *I am now a non-smoker. I feel great generally and I'm rapidly getting over the symptoms of withdrawal. I'm seeing a bit more money, a fitter me. I don't see the surprise and/or disgust from some people when they discovered that I was a smoker. Food has a new-found pleasure, sex too. Day-to-day travelling is a lot easier as I'm no longer constantly searching furtively for somewhere where I can have a quiet cigarette.*
>
> *What's particularly exciting is that now I am a non-smoker I have discovered some new friends. Most exciting is that my partner and I have a whole new better relationship and I know that getting promotion at work is going to be easier.*
>
> *Above all I feel I've reclaimed me: I've stopped feeling so pathetic about the whole thing.*

Step 3: Give ATTENTION at STRATEGIC level

Selecting strategies to guarantee success
Premise: there is a way to get what we want – it is known as a strategy. We must identify the best strategy we can.

Our strategy for becoming a non-smoker has four areas of focus:

Focus 1
We are going to give the task of stopping massive attention: we're going to so over-load that it will happen. We're talking about a serious physiological addiction coupled with a lot of psychology about image,

relationship and stress management. There's some serious work to do. When giving up smoking, do not work on any other change at the same time, certainly assuming you are running a busy life and trying to do a job, look after the family, etc. Often when people decide to give up smoking it is part of a grand 'spring clean' or 'new year, new you' and they decide that they are going to improve many parts of their live. Excellent. But when things get tough in this change programme, as it will definitely do, then smoking will become a comfort. For that reason address stopping smoking only. THEN work on other areas.

Focus 2

We are going to gain explicit pain/pleasure understanding. We must get beyond the logic of smoking being 'bad for you'. We all know that. In fact that message has been a part of our culture now for around 40 years. But what we're told in our school biology lessons and the side of cigarette packets DOES NOT STACK UP WITH WHAT WE SEE ON A DAY-TO-DAY BASIS. On a day-to-day basis most smokers we see – particularly in the media – look cool, seem perfectly normal, are often sexy and poised. And he/she is certainly not obviously suffering from lung cancer or heart disease. Smokers are often calm. Smokers are often individuals. Smokers are often role models. We've got to get back to basics and be clear in our own mind why smoking is NOT for us. We'll obviously do this in our pain/pleasure section.

Focus 3

We are going to break all the positive triggers to and associations with smoking. Every time we smoke we get benefit: 'Smoking may be bad for me, but it gives me a lot of pleasure too. It allows me to take short regular breaks'. 'It reminds me to take breaks'. 'It is a mini-meditation where I can be alone with the world'. 'It is a friendly habit'. 'It is a conspiratorial habit'. 'It is a reminder of when men were men and women were women. The cowboy around the camp-fire: the romantic swirl of cigar smoke'. 'It's symbolic of the true martyr – last request: a cigarette.'

Focus 4

And a final focus will be to encourage you to smoke, but to smoke properly. Yes, go ahead. Do smoke. But smoke *consciously* in a *sensory-rich* way. If you must smoke, then do it properly! Don't worry, there's reason in our madness!

Step 4: Give ATTENTION at TACTICAL level

Getting tactial to ensure vision into action
Premise: we must turn our strategy into day-to-day tactics which are easily implemented.

This is where we get our strategy to happen: the high level areas of focus are broken down into achievable detail.

Focus 1
Give it massive attention. When you make the decision to become a non-smoker – *and now would be a good time to do that* – *work only on this personal change.* Of course if you feel it does help to take up swimming, perhaps because it makes you feel better or it distracts you, then excellent, But if taking up swimming is another struggle, forget it for the moment. Your sole focus must be on becoming a non-smoker. You do not want to be distracted from this task. Your day-to-day priority will be the process of becoming a non-smoker. This does not mean we will always be thinking about smoking: clearly that could be counter-productive. No, what it means is that our brain and body are working on that process, alone.

Focus 2
Explicit pain/pleasure identification. This is so critical that we will look at this separately: see step 6

Focus 3
Break all the positive triggers. Smoking is typically a background activity: it supports us while we are doing something else; even a 'quiet smoke' is actually a support for us having a reflective think. We are generally smoking while we are doing something else: talking,

drinking a beer, watching TV, relaxing after sex, even thinking. These are all intensely positive activities. Not only are we creating an intensively positive association with the action of smoking, we are not fully 'aware' of our smoking. The creation of a positive association we will look at now. The lack of 'awareness' we will look at in focus 4.

So, our task is to break all the positive triggers. We do this by noting what they are for us and then replacing them with a more positive association. For example, if having a cigarette creates a feeling of peacefulness and allows us to take a break and relax, we must find an alternative for that.

Here are the top six triggers and how we tackle them: in every case we must create a replacement for the state provided if we are going to achieve the change we are looking for.

- **Companionship.** Taking a cigarette break is companionship. Lighting up with others is companionship. *Replace this with:* Deliberately associate with friends who are non-smokers. And/or buddy up with a smoker who also wishes to give up. Go for a walk when others go for a smoke. Avoid situations where you will end up with a crowd of smokers.
- **Image.** Who are your image-makers? The cowboys, there out on the range? Humphrey Bogart? A current rock star? A young fashion model? *Replace this with:* Other role models. Those whose image is emphasised by their skill rather than their smoking. Deliberately up-date your own personal rock stars and image-makers.
- **Martyr.** Yeah I know. Life is tough, isn't it? And smoking is one of your last simple pleasures. But maybe that's as much a mindset. *Replace this with:* How about getting your relationship back online and getting down to the gym and being nice to your parents and kids and sorting out your career? And maybe as you did that you'd notice that life isn't so bad.
- **Stress release.** At last, that cigarette: it helps so much at those tricky times. And it's always there: in the pocket, in the handbag, available. *Replace that with:* Learn a simple meditation. Take up yoga.

Take more lunch-time walks at work.
- **Being sexy.** I know. It's very French, very European. It keeps you slim, it allows you to pose. But have you kissed someone who stinks of smoke? Or who stinks of smoke slightly disguised with mint? It's not sexy. Smoking is not sexy. *Replace this with:* Developing who you are. Learning about yourself. Developing your authenticity.
- **Reflection:** You've used it as an excuse for a break. As a mini-meditation. To punctuate the day. *Replace this with:* Do a proper meditation. Develop your assertiveness skills so that you don't need an excuse.

Focus 4

Smoke consciously, in line with our approach of not ignoring smoking but alternatively bringing it right into our conscious. Whenever you smoke, stop everything else. Light up carefully. As you inhale, notice how it feels and what it is doing to your lungs. Now notice at an even deeper level what it is doing to your lungs. Whenever a thought comes to mind about smoking, bring it fully into consciousness and cognitively wrestle with it. Remind yourself that you are only smoking because of one of the triggers (see focus 3). If you have to lose in that wrestle, then smoke consciously. Note that we are not trying to 'forget' smoking, but alternatively, specifically *remember* that we are doing it.

Step 5: Create IMMERSION at BRAIN level

Getting resourceful

Premise: although many do give 'attention' to the change they seek, most then move on before the change is completed. We don't fall into that trap. We ensure we immerse ourselves in the change so that the change becomes irreversible.

We should at this stage have a strong inclination to stop smoking as we have already (1) created an empowered mindset to support us in this work (2) created a vivid and explicit mental model of what we are seeking (3) identified a strategy which will give us success (4) high-lighted the tactics which are necessary to ensure the change happens.

We can now reinforce that by:

- **Looking after yourself.** This is going to be a potentially tough time. Your body and brain are seeped in noxious chemicals. And if that weren't bad enough, your body has reached a steady state with those chemicals and we now want to detox the body. To aid the process:
  - Take time out – walk, swim, read. If some activities are ones you would associate with smoking such as reading, then find a place such as the library where you can read but can't smoke. This will help build up your new association.
  - Get extra sleep.
  - Eat very well. Reintroduce a proper range of foods if your diet had been poor, particularly if smoking has been a 'weight loss crutch'. Focus on fruit and vegetables.

- **Run these affirmations.** An affirmation is quick mind-set adjustment. When it gets tough, run one of these statements:
  - I am > addictions.
  - I am > marketing efforts of the tobacco industry.
  - I am > the unhelpful comment of my friends.

- **Keep busy.** When you want to take a break, do so, but do it with an 'activity' such as meditation or walking or going to a coffee shop and chatting.

- **Note progress.**

Step 6: Create IMMERSION at EMOTION level

Using the pain/pleasure lever

Of all the desires we have, the lever is probably most crucial for this one. Of all our desires this is the one with most physical addiction. So our cognitive, rational 'change ability' is going to have to be very good.

Once again, time for you to do some serious work. You need pen and paper or keyboard and screen. Here are your questions:

Q1: What will you gain by the becoming a non-smoker? Write quickly and without stopping. What is it specifically that you will gain? What attracts you about finally giving up smoking?

....

....

....

....

That's good. But there's more than that of course. You won't just look and feel good and have more energy. Your skin is going to start to repair and reverse the aging process which smoking has started. You are going to look younger and more attractive. What else will you gain by this change?

....

....

....

....

Q2: Why haven't you changed? What pleasures are you clinging onto as a smoker?

....

....

....

....

No – more honesty needed. Are you concerned that you may never feel 'satisfied' again? That you'll lose that little ritual of 'quiet moments'? That it helps you in those social moments of where to put your hands? Does it bring pleasure to that long commute back home?

....

....

....

....

Q3: What pain do you associate with making the change?

....

....

....

....

That's true, but what about maintaining it for ever more, not just for the next few months? And you know, don't you, that you do tend to react quite badly and get coughs, etc, when you give up. And you do tend to put on weight.

....

....

....

....

Q4: What will be the cost if you don't make the change? You need to get very explicit on this one.

....

....

....

....

What exactly? What will happen to your health? To your feelings about yourself? It's not so good, is it? What exactly is happening to your lungs and to your heart? And what are the consequences of that?

....

....

....

....

Come on, be honest, it's worse than that. What actually will happen to you? And what implications will that have for the future? Your career? Your family?

Step 7: Create IMMERSION at STRATEGIC level

Break and date

Now review your strategy. Review your pain/pleasure responses. Break your plans down into small, measurable actions. Actions which are brain- and time-friendly. And make them time and date specific. You'll decide yours. Here are some example ones:

Anne

Anne had smoked since she was a teenager. It was how she managed her weight. But having said that at age 32 she knew it was getting pretty serious and if she didn't find an alternative way of managing her weight soon, she was going to have serious problems. Here was her break and break:

Of my 2.5 weeks annual holiday, the first week is going to be absolutely dedicated to giving up smoking. During that week:

- Any smoking will be fully conscious.
- I have booked two massages, using money saved from smoking.
- I will concentrate on eating really well.
- I have put the reasons that I don't want to smoke any longer on the fridge door.

I have also:
- Calculated how much I will save when I stop and I dearly want that money;
- Shouted at my boyfriend (in the nicest possible way of course) that if he doesn't want to join me in giving up, that's fine but he does need to stop trying to break my strategies.

Pablo

It was particularly hard for Pablo. Coming from Spain where the culture was still pretty ambivalent about smoking it was harder to avoid smoking and the offer of cigarettes. Here was his plan:
- Find two other people who are absolutely serious about giving up smoking too.
- Decider to allocate the first week's spend to a charity.
- Whenever he craved a smoke at work, he was going to walk outside and get 10 minutes fresh air. Whenever he craved a cigarette at home he was going to put on some loud rock music and dance around the place a bit. In both cases he was of course trying to 'over-write' the association.

Deirdre

Deirdre loved her home country of Ireland. But boy did they love their drink, cigarettes and gossip. But the opportunity came when the country decided to ban smoking in bars; she decided to go for it too at that time. She just stopped. No other fuss. Just stopped. She just decided to have a mindset that she was going to be greater than this addiction, she was going to stop her silly little fantasy about being more 'French' through her smoking. She was going to grow up.

Step 8: Create TACTICS at IMMERSION level

Commit to plan

Premise: when what we need to do is visible, it is more likely to happen.

Get it onto your wall planner: up on the wall and in every diary you need. Make it clear and bold. In particular ensure you schedule real time, i.e. support group review 7-7.30pm not just '7'.

Here are some tips:

- Ensure the planner is visible. Create some kind of progress area if at all possible: a bit of the kitchen cork-board. In your workshop or study if you have one. This is a project, treat it as such.
- Ensure you have both a big bold visible version where you can see at a glance the progress made and in particular your 'keep busy' activities; and a portable one which is always with you.
- Mark it with clear graphics and pictures.
- Importantly, celebrate successes with big ticks or smileys; whatever is your style. 1 day without smoking. 10 days without smoking. 100 days without smoking. 250 days without smoking. First family holiday without smoking. First interview for new job without smoking.
- If you are in a buddy set-up: have rewards and celebration but not counter to the hard work you are doing. E.g. don't reward three days of not smoking with a cigar. You laugh: it happens!
- Have lots of measurables, such as amount of money saved, number of smoke breaks not taken.
- On all your planners have simple summary statements written which state what you want to do and why you are trying to do it.

Step 9: Create MOMENTUM at BRAIN level

Pareto power

Premise: with any change there are a few things we can always do which will give us a high pay-off. Don't necessarily try to do everything as you may consequently do nothing.

What are the high pay-offs that will ensure you kick this habit?

1. *Decide* to give up smoking. You must have said it to yourself. You must have written it down somewhere. You must have made it conscious. Too often it is vague 'maybes' 'I'm hoping', etc. Not acceptable. This is a pronouncement, a declaration, a personal contract, a binding agreement, a test of your integrity, your authenticity, your manhood, your femininity, your true you. This is it.
2. *Concentrate only* on giving up smoking. One change at a time. This is

so potentially powerful, it does need massive attention. And when we are working on other changes we tend to compensate by saying, at least I got my tax return in at last so I guess I deserve a smoke. So, becoming a non-smoker is the key.

3. *Break* all connections which lead to smoking. And ensure every one has a clear positive replacement. Every single one. If you don't get replacements, smoking will be back.

4. Keep the costs of *not changing* clear. And more than clear, make them frightening.

5. *Create* a support team. But the best. The ones who will support you as much as you will support them.

Step 10: Create MOMENTUM at EMOTION level

Breaking the pattern
Premise: our conditioning may well be long and hard with an old habit. A pattern break or a pattern interrupt takes us out of that mould and gives us a chance to build new neural networks and new muscle memories.

Remember the purpose of a pattern break. So if some of these seem harsh, radical, challenging, that's the reason! Try these:

Break the pattern by:
- Committing your annual spend on cigarettes *up front* to your favourite charity. And let several people know you've done it. And fill in the standing order form to the charity. And post it. Frightening? Sure, but nothing compared to debilitating lung cancer or heart disease at age 37.
- Start now; no more planning. You thought you would start when you had finished the book. No. Start now. No, don't even wait until the end of this section. Start now. Too pushy? Nothing compared to the pressure your young children will be under when they lose a parent.
- Get a detailed advanced medical book on the effects of smoking. Study and learn it as if you were medical student. Learn the jargon.

Become a guru on the really nasty pernicious effects of smoking. Copy that photo of what it does to your lungs. Stick it on the fridge. Photocopy that picture of a patient with tubes in his throat. Put it in your wallet where you will see it every day.
■ Agree a series of simple treats as a reward for yourself when you don't smoke. Build in an 'accelerator'. E.g. 1 day, trip to cinema; 3 days, massage; 10 days, trip to theatre; 30 days, day trip to Paris, etc.
■ Look at yourself in the mirror and give yourself a talking to 'if you can't beat this..., you're frankly pathetic...'.

And create your own. Just how radical can you be?

Step 11: Getting a STRATEGY at MOMENTUM level

Breaking through
Premise: we're so close to getting what we want. What is going to stop us? Who is going to stop us? Are there any final blockers? Identify them. Solve them.

So, what's going to stop you? The big three will be:
■ Pure addiction; pure chemical addiction. Molecule to molecule. Length of neural network steeped in addictive stuff.
■ The attractions that smoking brings you: friendship, stress management, quiet moments to think, something to do with your hands.
■ Personal relationships who feel threatened by the change you are going to make.

All of these you know you can resolve. We've discussed how to. You know how to. Here's the real answer to the question – *the only blocker to this is you.* Decide now that you are going to do it. Forget terms such as will-power and self-discipline. These are just jargon terms to hide behind. Further reasons for putting it off. Now is the time to JfDI!

Step 12: Bold first steps

Take it away!

Premise: there comes a point when we talk no more, we study no more, we plan no more: we start, we take action we do something. We get on the path to the success we want. That is the very essence of JfDI! So: JfDI! Just Do It.

So, now is the time to take those bold steps: there is no more thinking, no more study, no more discussion. It's 'get on with it' time. What have you decided if you haven't started work already? Have you assembled your support team? Have you committed this month's smoking expenditure in advance to your favourite charity? Have you had your last cigarette? Have you dedicated the next fortnight to this task? Here are some bold steps you might wish to try:

1. Do something now which will get you on the path to being a non-smoker.
2. Ring up some friends or talk to some colleagues and create your support team.
3. Do some arithmetic: how much you could save and what you could do with the money. Get detailed with the figures.
4. Plan your evenings for the next two weeks so that you will be out and busy and not craving a cigarette; remember you'll have a bit more money to play with for socialising.
5. Search the house for anything smoking-related: ashtrays, lighters, even packets of mints and air-fresheners. Even the mug for your tea which 'goes with' the early morning smoke. Chuck it all in the bin. Now.
6. Become a volunteer at the local hospital and offer to work with cancer patients.
7. Commit to someone you love and trust about your decision and ask for their help. Ask them to be empathetic, but not sympathetic.
8. Start, start, start.

Things to do

Step 1: Choose brilliant, supporting mindsets. How about 'I can beat the seducers', those being (1) the nicotine chemicals streaming in my blood-stream and (2) the marketers?

Step 2: Create the most powerful VEMM ever. It's you: looking very, very fit. And more importantly, you *are* very, very fit. Smoking is a thing of the past and it has helped you moderate other pastimes such as drinking which were getting a little out of control. No signs of smoking. No smells of smoking. And life is very good for you. No chemical, no marketing campaign manages you. You do: you are a free person.

Step 3: What's the strategy you will give most focus to? Start with being conscious of your smoking, support that with *breaking* the triggers.

Step 4: What are the critical tactics to support that strategy? Start breaking in detail every single trigger which takes you back to the cigarette. Keep finding the connections, the routes which take you back. Break them.

Step 5: Are you inclined to act? Get so you are. You'll need sleep, good nutrition and gentle exercise to build fitness and immune system. Get to it. Now.

Step 6: Have you worked your pain/pleasure lever? Are you clear in what's going to happen if this change doesn't happen? Really clear? It's not all that good, is it? As long as you know. But what will be the fantastic benefits?

Step 7: Have you broken it down, and broken it down. Make it so easy, so attractive that you can get it done? Do that now.

Step 8: Is it 'in yer face'? How often per day will it be?

Step 9: What's the high pay-off? Good.

Step 10: How can you once and for all break the pattern? What can you do radically differently?

Step 11: Only you will stop you. Got that?

Step 12: Start. Now.

NB's thoughts

Physical addictions are hard: smoking, alcohol, drugs. Hard because of the physical, chemical connection with our bodies and hard because of the many, many secondary reasons that cause us to smoke, such as sociability, sex, stress management... Or cause us to start on the slippery slope of excess alcohol or even drugs.

Notice carefully when you begin to 'crave' certain foods. Even chocolate and coffee; keep them as a pleasure, not 'things to keep me going'.

For me, my biggest breakthrough in this area was breaking secondary connections. My addiction was alcohol. Wine drinking is an easy pleasure. Choosing special spirits such as whisky or increasingly vodkas is an easy pastime. But it doesn't take long before a simple pleasure becomes a necessity and then an addiction.

There are many who cannot get through an evening without their bottle of wine or two. Their rationalisations are many: they deserve it; it's been a tough day; there aren't many simple pleasures left. Break free. You are not an addict: you are a free person!

Desire 3: To write and publish a book

Desire 1 (To lose weight, get fit, feel well and attractive) and Desire 2 (To give up smoking) perhaps fall into the category of 'have to's' for an individual. That doesn't make them any less desirable, but there is often a feeling for an individual that they 'have' to do them. Desire 3 is perhaps a little different. No one 'has' to write a book. This desire truly does come under the heading of wish or desire. And it's an excellent one to consider: so often an individual feels it would be so amazing to get their book written; it's a passion. But it's also a desire which we need to clarify. Because without this clarification, the personal change – the writing of the book – is unlikely to happen. For example, if your reason for writing a book is in order to become wealthy, perhaps think again. There are probably easier strategies. And a better strategy might be to identify that you wish to make extra money and consider which routes to that extra wealth might exist.

Let's also be clear that there are two distinct strategies bundled here: one is to write a book, to become a writer, the second is to get the book published. And notice the critical concept here: the real thing is to become a writer. To write and to get published we need to become *a writer.*

Step 1: Give ATTENTION at BRAIN level

Adjusting your mindset to support your change
Fundamental premise: mindset dictates behaviours which dictate results, so develop a supportive mindset.

Here are some potential empowering mindsets to adopt in our desire to write and publish a book, in our quest to become a writer:

- *I have a story.* We do all have stories: partly-formed, buried away there in our brain. Some are based on our experiences, some are pure imagination. We all have stories and people like stories so some people will be keen to read your story. It is the basis of a novel.
- *I have an imagination.* You couldn't have got this far if you weren't a possibility thinker. So you can image some scenarios, some stories, some characters and use those as basis for your book.
- *I have a skill or specific knowledge for a non-fiction book.* And yes, no doubt it will have been done before. That means there is a market out there yearning for more or requiring a different slant: you can provide that.
- *I can write, in my style.* No you don't have Hemingway's style or the flow of Jane Austen or the wackiness of a modern author. But neither did they originally and neither attempted to copy someone else's style. Your style must be yours. And your style will be what a potential publisher is looking for.
- *I can get feedback and improve.* There'll be no end of feedback for you and that's an opportunity to improve.
- *I can do it for enjoyment.* Whatever happens, enjoy your writing and focus on the pleasure it gives you. Of course there will be hard sessions where the book seems to be falling apart and you feel it will never make any progress, but in the long term you will get there and therefore you can enjoy it.
- *I am a writer.* This is probably the most fundamental one, when one day we allow ourselves to acknowledge that we are a writer.
- *I can get it published.* But if the quest was to become a writer you can genuinely allow that to be a secondary issue.

Here are some limiting mindsets to put aside:
- *I'll never get published.* You will. You simply need to get to reach an appropriate standard and then persist. Both of those, you can do. You will get published; there is a match between you, the book and a publisher. It's simply finding it.
- *My ideas won't be good enough.* If they are not, then ask for feedback and improve.
- *My style isn't right.* You can learn through doing and getting feedback and reading those who are getting published at the moment.

Step 2: Give ATTENTION at EMOTION level

Getting passionate and creating a vivid, explicit, mental model
Premise: we must get engagement at heart and gut level as well as at brain and intellectual level. Here we create a vivid, explicit mental model.

Question 1: What do you want?
We need some honesty here. This of all the desires. Why *do* you want to write? Why *do* you want to publish? Think about it and jot down your thoughts:

....

....

....

....

Was it any of these?
- For fun.
- To change the world.
- To make some money.
- To make a point.
- For status.
- For a new career.
- It's something I can do while bringing up young children.
- I just want to try it; there's a lot of rubbish out there and I reckon I can do it better.
- I have one book in me; it's bursting to get out.

You must be honest. Because some of those reasons will certainly help you write your book. But let's be honest: some of them are going to hinder you. With some of them, is writing a book the best route to achieve your true goal?

Which will probably help?
- For fun. If you do it for fun, you are doing it for excellent reasons. There is a sense of light-heartedness, you are not being too precious about the process and you can cope with the set-backs.
- To change the world. This is good too. You've probably got plenty of passion lined up in there.
- To make a point. True also. You feel strongly about something; you want to make that point.

Which will possibly hinder?
- To make some money. You probably won't. Not with this goal. Most of the (few) authors who have become wealthy have done so, simply by setting out to write a good book. And then it really takes off. Even if your book is acknowledged to be a 'best-seller' you may not be making enough to give up the day job. If you simply want to become wealthy you may want to think seriously about an alternative strategy. But if that reality check doesn't put you off then you've probably got what it takes.
- For status. This might be easier to achieve than wealth, but, perhaps a better question would be to understand the psychology behind this. Why do you want 'status'?

Which could go either way?
- For a new career. As long as you don't treat it as many people treat their career, i.e. just as something they 'do'. Writing requires serious engagement and a full use of all of your abilities: you need to get fully involved.
- It's something I can do while bringing up young children. True, but choose it because you want to write a book, not because you need to.
- I just want to try it; there's a lot of rubbish out there and I reckon I can do it better. Excellent: you probably can.

So, just check the reason you want it. Maybe there's an easier way. But if you're choosing it for a good reason, excellent.

Question 2: Imagine you now have what you want. You are now an author. Your book is out. What are you seeing? What is the cover of your book like? Where are you when you see the first copy? Which is the first local book shop in which you see a copy? What is the headline of the first review?

....

....

....

....

Are you doing book signings, or do you hate those? Where are you noticing your book? Did you see someone on the tube the other day reading it?

....

....

....

....

And what else are you seeing?

....

....

....

....

Question 3: You now have what you want, what are you hearing?

....

....

....

....

What's the feedback been like? What have the marketing team been saying about the book? Are they pleased? Is there talk of commissioning you to do another book?

And what else are you hearing? What questions are being asked in your first radio interview? How were you introduced on air? You have some very supportive friends who have encouraged you to write this book, what are they saying as you give them their first signed copy?

....

....

....

....

Question 4: You now have what you want, what are you feeling? What are your feelings as you finally see a copy of your book?

....

....

....

....

Tired? Exhilarated? Annoyed with stupid journalist questions? Fed up because no one is buying it? Amazed at how many old friends have contacted you?

Once you have finished writing, review your notes.

Now pull it all together so that you have around 500 words of sensory rich description detailing exactly your new life. It'll obviously be your description, but maybe it'll be something like this:

> *I am now a writer. Most days I write. Initially I just wrote character sketches, bits of plot, but now I am writing my first novel. I am feeling really good about it, especially as I have struggled for years with this wish and now finally it is just*

happening. I've had some early comments from friends who I know would give an honest view and they like it. This coming week I'm planning to spend some time in Borders bookshop looking at publishers doing stuff in my area with a view to sending my first proposals. I need to find out about agents: do I need one, I'm not sure?

My long-term aim is certainly to give up my day job and become a full-time writer. But I have to say just doing this amount of writing is helping make the rest of my life more enjoyable.

Step 3: Give ATTENTION at STRATEGIC level

Selecting strategies to guarantee success

Premise: there is a way to get what we want – it is known as a strategy. We must identify the best strategy we can.

There are two strategies we need (1) we need one for writing the book and (2) we need one for getting the book published. A challenge is that they are quite different strategies. For example, the writing element needs a degree of solitude, a degree of introversion. Whereas getting published needs a little commercialism, a willingness to 'expose' oneself and be rejected – often many, many times. So, let's understand both:

Strategy for writing the book
Here are the seven keys for getting your writing to happen, for becoming a writer and producing your book.

1. Your overall most fundamental not-to-be-forgotten point is that you must write. Every day and for as long as you can every day. And that might mean at odd times and in odd places. You must write. As well as obviously producing words, writing clarifies your thinking and improves and aids future writing; writing helps writing. So write. And when you write you aid the transition to becoming a writer. It is easy to write when you are a writer, just as it is easy to garden when you are a gardener. But if you are still 'a

mum', yes it is difficult to write. If you are still an 'account manager', yes it is difficult to write. So write: to produce, to develop, to become a writer.

2. Schedule your writing time. I'm sorry, I know you're an artist and you need to wait for inspiration. Hey, you could be a long time waiting. Inspiration tends to come when we actually start writing. Simply putting pen to paper, fingers to keyboard will produce the inspiration. Aim for 45-90 minute chunks of time. Longer if you can and certainly several times a day, if you can. Don't begrudge just 30 minutes on your laptop on the train. It's all writing.

3. Get into state. You must feel refreshed and focused. Work can be produced when fatigued, when anxious, but it's unlikely to be your best work when in that mode. Look after yourself. Get your sleep. Eat properly. Take walks and time out. Keep talking to people.

4. And now we can combine the two previous concepts to discover one of the breakthroughs of great writing: writing plus state = flow state. Flow state is high productivity with minimum apparent effort. Write: simply write and keep the flow going and slip into flow state. Importantly at this stage do not judge your work and to a certain extent, see where the writing takes you.

5. Have editing periods after writing. Not pre-writing. When your energy is flagging, when you have slipped out of flow state. Do a spell-check. Do some severe editing. Then leave it and get on with another section.

6. When writing in flow state: don't judge, just produce. When editing do basic correction and add detail. In fiction, not just *the detective arrived*, but *the inspector dropped his briefcase to the floor as he accepted the mug of warming tea.* In non-fiction, help the reader with your ideas: to use them, to learn them.

7. But what do you write about? You write about what you want to write about. Because if you do you will write well and people will want to read it. Don't write about what you don't want to write about, simply because you think it is 'clever' or there is a 'market' out there. Which is why it is important to be clear on why you want to write and why writing for the simple reason of 'becoming wealthy' rarely works whereas the process of simply writing does occasionally produce wealthy writers.

Strategy for getting it published

Here are the seven keys for getting published:

1. Recognise that publishers in general do want to discover new good authors. It is true that many, if not all, are inundated with proposals. But a lot of these are poor quality, many atrociously bad. So your challenge is allowing time (often months) for your proposal to get to the top of the pile and when it does to ensure it is given more than 30 seconds of study.

2. You must put together a proposal. That will vary slightly depending on whether you are proposing non-fiction or fiction. Check with the 'targeted' publisher, in what format they prefer their proposal; increasingly publishers detail what they are looking for on their website. One or two at any particular time may say they are not currently accepting any more work.

3. When writing your proposal, think publisher. The publisher needs to know why this book will sell. Bottom line, that is what they are about. They may be sympathetic to your cause. They might enjoy the twist in the story. But will it sell? Now of course publishers make mistakes as they are busy, so you need to influence them as much as possible. Here are some ways:
    - Clarity of presentation. Is what you are offering clear? Have you followed their house rules for presentation of material?
    - Ease of contact with you. They may have some immediate questions – can they e-mail you, ring you?
    - A sample or manuscript: double-spaced.

4. No gimmicks. Seriously. Publishers have seen them all and they're not amused!

5. Keep detailed records of who you approach and how you approach. You will get some suggestions from some publishers even if they don't take on your book. You can follow up at a later date. Be courteous at all times. Many publishers recognise that even though they reject you now, you might have a great offer in the future.

6. Keep at it; be persistent. Don't be frightened of ringing one or two if they show some interest and then it goes quiet for some time. But don't hassle them.

7. In the meantime, keep writing.

Step 4: Give ATTENTION at TACTICAL level

Getting tactical to ensure vision into action

Premise: we must turn our strategy into day-to-day tactics which are easily implementable.

Here are the seven paradoxical tactics of great writing to use for your book. Adapt them to your own requirements:

Paradox 1: Create a writing ritual. But break it often!

It's generally easier to get down to work and write when there is an established ritual that you can sink into. When your desk is ready, and it is uncluttered. The laptop is there. The pad of paper and pencils. It's not too hot and it's not too cold. Everything is within reach: some water, some fruit. Because when you sit down you'll slide into the seat of a writer, and you know that's what you are intended to do, so you might as well get on with it: write.

If for that reason you can make it a dedicated location which is only for your writing and not the place you pay your bills, that would be excellent. Try hard to build up a positive association with your writing area.

But it's like the toddler who can only sleep with teddy, the lady who can't jog without her iPod. Don't let these rituals get too strong; I want you to be able to write anywhere. So do so: the garden, the kitchen table, the library, a local cafe. In the train and at the airport.

Paradox 2: Write every day. But take time out.

You've got to put the time in. Who ever did anything worthwhile without putting the time in? Roger Bannister, M Raymond Blanc, the Beatles – the great put the time in. You'll need to do so to. So write every day. Identify your best times of the day. If you're a morning person, get up, have a slice of toast and a drink and write for 90 minutes. Have breakfast; go for a further two hours. That's the way to do it. If you're an evening person or an afternoon person, same idea. At the end of a working session, as you are probably beginning to wind down, take ten minutes to get sorted out and prepared for the next day. Run the spell check. Up-date your yellow sticky on the overall plan of your book.

But don't get dull. Writing – as with any art, be it sculpture or people management – is not something to be 'machined'. You must take some time out and relax and view how to do things differently. To allow the neural network to look at things in a different way.

Paradox 3: Write long and fast without judgement. But edit hard.

When you write, when you type, generally do it quickly. Allow yourself to slip into that flow state, that state at which your most powerful work appears. Do that by writing fast, by writing hard, by not judging your work, by ensuring that everything is being captured as you think it. And trust it will be good. And it will be.

But you must edit hard. You'll discover endless paragraphs which are perfect, which are a delight to read. But some you'll find a little frustrating. That's OK, you can edit them. And one or two that are rubbish. That's OK, 'delete' takes only a micro-second.

Paradox 4: Measure quantity. But focus on quality.

Decide an overall word count. Distribute it as best you can across the structure of your book – an approximate number per chapter say, or per topic in a non-fiction book. Work hard to hit your word count on a daily basis.

But do everything you can to maintain quality: stay fresh, take breaks when it seems to be hard day. Respect your mood if you are a little 'under the weather'.

And do your editing.

Paradox 5: Ensure data deprivation. But read the best.

You need to get your ideas out. Too much input can stop that. Be careful with too much perusal of the daily newspaper or books or TV. Allow time for your ideas to develop without being 'bettered'. Allow time for them to 'knit' together. This we call 'data deprivation' time.

But when you do read, read the best. Don't worry; as long as your own writing is strong they won't strangle your own style.

Paradox 6: Above all, write. But what?

If it's fiction, it's what's in your head. It's your story. Just write. As you write it will unfold. You'll probably have an overall idea of where you are going but trust that characters will develop as you write.

If it's non-fiction, adopt the same approach as far as you can. Of course you will need to refer to data and research. But your writing will be more elegant if you form an overall cogent picture for the reader.

Tactics

Here are the tactics for getting your book published:

- Write your proposal as you start writing your book. This will clarify in your mind what book you are writing. Yes, the book may well change significantly as you start to write it so you can always adjust your proposal, but it's best to keep them in synch, especially if you are seeking a very commercial proposition.
- Start early with your proposals. Particularly with non-fiction books, publishers do not expect a completed manuscript, so start getting your book in the proposal piles.
- Give reasons for success.

Step 5: Create IMMERSION at BRAIN level

Getting resourceful

Premise: although many do give 'attention' to the change they seek, most then move on before the change is completed. We don't fall into that trap. We ensure we immerse ourselves in the change so that the change becomes irreversible.

We should at this stage have a strong inclination to act as we have already (1) created an empowered mindset to support us in this work (2) created a vivid and explicit mental model of what we are seeking (3) identified a strategy which will give us success (4) highlighted the tactics which are necessary to ensure the change happens.

We can reinforce that by:

- Looking after ourselves – taking time out, getting sleep and getting data deprivation time;
- By using the following affirmations:
    - I am > pulls in other directions.
    - I am > negative feedback from others.
    - I have a story with me.
    - I am an expert in my niche.

When writing a book, especially if it is not 'our career', especially if it is not crucially needed for funding, then structure to our writing is vital. Create a simple timetable and stick to it.

Step 6: Create IMMERSION at EMOTION level

Using the pain/pleasure lever

Once again, time for you to do some serious work. You need pen and paper or keyboard and screen. Here are your questions:

Q1: What will you gain by this change? Write quickly and without stopping. What is it that you will gain? What attracts you about writing and publishing a book?

....

....

....

....

Come on, there's more than that. It won't just be exciting. It will be tremendous; so many people want to write a book and they never get around to it. But you're not going to be one of those people. You're going to get it done. And it's got to make it easier with any other ambitions you have. Once you've run your first marathon, everything is easier. What else will you gain by this change?

....

....

....

....

Being honest, is it also about 'proving' yourself, perhaps? So, what else?

Q2: Why haven't you changed? What pleasure do you get from where you are? Let's be direct; why haven't you written that book? What pleasure do you get from the non-writing? What are you doing instead?

....

....

....

....

No – more honesty needed. Are you concerned that you'll get adverse criticism or that it will not be a best-seller?

....

....

....

....

Or is it something practical such as no decent lap-top for your work?

Q3: What pain do you associate with making the change?

....

....

....

....

That's true, but what about if the book is a flop? Doesn't sell many? Does that trouble you? Or if it gets some bad reviews? Come on, be honest. What's troubling you about making that change?

....

....

....

....

Q4: What will be the cost if we don't make the change? You need to get very explicit with this one.

....

....

....

....

What exactly? How will you feel about yourself? Do think you'll ever really feel proud about not having done it?

....

....

....

....

Step 7: Create IMMERSION at STRATEGIC level

Break and date

Now review your strategy. Review your pain/pleasure responses. Break your plans down into small, measurable actions. Actions which are brain- and time-friendly. And make them time and date specific. You'll decide yours. Here are some example ones:

Lucy's actions

Non-fiction book on gardening

- Write every morning for 45 minutes, before leaving for work. Do it whatever my mood.
- Edit/expand my previous evening and morning writing every lunch-time for 30 minutes. Do it however busy I am at work.
- Write every evening for 60 mins. Research/read for 30 mins.
- Ensure Friday evening and all Saturday as a rest period.
- Restrict TV viewing. Cancel newspaper.
- Create dedicated writing area and move off kitchen table.
- Write on the fridge 'I am a writer'.

Peter's actions

Detective novel

- Write the outline plot on a flip-chart sheet on study wall.
- Allocate the approximate number of words to each section of the plot.
- Aim for 1 chapter per week: novel completed in approx 3 months.
- Write during week: at week-ends plan approach to agents to represent book.
- Spend time on tube making jottings to develop characters.

Sara's actions

Travel guide with food emphasis: Paris

- Book a cheap week-end to Paris.
- Write the framework to the book while there to capture the enthusiasm for the place: over the three day week-end, visit six *arrondisements* and do a different meal in each.

Step 8: Create TACTICS at IMMERSION level

Commit to plan

Get it onto you wall planner: up on the wall and in every diary you need. Make it clear and bold. In particular ensure you schedule real time, i.e. write 8-10 not just 8.

Here are some tips:

- Ensure the planner is visible, not hidden in the back bedroom.
- Ensure you have both a big bold visible version and a portable one.
- Mark it with clear graphics and pictures.
- Importantly, celebrate successes with big ticks or smileys; whatever is your style.
- If you are in a buddy set-up: have rewards and celebrations but not counter to the hard work you are doing. E.g. don't celebrate a week's successful writing with two weeks off.
- If at all possible, create a progress chart: characters developed, words written, chapters written.

Step 9: Create MOMENTUM at BRAIN level

Pareto power

Premise: with any change there are a few things we can always do which will give us a high pay-off. Don't necessarily try to do everything as you may consequently do nothing.

Incredibly simple: write!

The Pareto factor for a writer is so simple, so straightforward. There is simply no debate about it. You must write and you must write every day. And that's it. And if you say but I don't know what to write or... Then see what's blocking you, below.

Step 10: Create MOMENTUM at EMOTION level

Breaking the pattern

Premise: our conditioning may well be long and hard with an old habit. A pattern break or a pattern interrupt take us out of that mould and gives us a chance to build new neural networks and new muscle memories.

Five ways to break the pattern of a non-writer:

- Decide to write just 100 words of your opening chapter. Now.
- Go back to some earlier work: re-work it, edit it, expand it. Now.
- Record your first chapter on tape. If it works, maybe more of the novel can be done this way.
- *Draw* the plot on art paper. Now write about your drawing.
- Go to the library and write. Now.

Step 11: Getting a STRATEGY at MOMENTUM level

Breaking through

Premise: we're so close to getting what we want. What is going to stop us? Are there any final blockers? Identify them. Solve them.

So, what's stopping you? Why the struggle? Let's take a look.

I don't know what to write.
Put pen to paper or fingers to keyboard and write and write and then continue. If necessary write 'I don't know what to write' 15 times. You will slip out of that unresourceful state. Look around for some inspiration. A newspaper heading. An ambulance siren going off in the distance.

I will start the book, but: when I retire/when the children leave home/the study is re-decorated, etc.
No, there will always be 'one more thing'. Start now.

I have money worries.
Take a day off from writing. Sort the financial concerns as best you can. Go and see the bank manager. Arrange a consolidation loan on the longest time period and lowest interest rate terms you can. Get a part-time teaching job. But address these concerns.

I have relationship worries.
Take a day off. Address them: ring who needs to be rung. Cry. Shout. Sort it out. You won't solve them in a day but you will begin to do so.

I have life worries.
Take a day off. Write down everything that is currently worrying you: one per line. Adjacent to the worry, write the next step you will take to resolve the issue. Do alternate days of writing and addressing the issues. You'll be delighted that you are making progress on both.

I'm an artist; I shouldn't be treated like this.
You may be an artist, but I'm afraid that doesn't give you any special treatment over the rest of us mere mortals. You have a craft, a job to do. And as with the rest of us mortals, you need to get on with it.

I have no time to write.
Take your diary, turn to the first free day. Book two one-hour slots for writing. No ifs or buts.

I have writer's block.
Stop using this term. In fact don't ever use it again. It's simply a label, an excuse and it's far too easy to drag out and say. That doesn't mean you'll always be at your best for writing, but be very careful of this oh-so-convenient label. If you feel it is genuine and not just 'celebrity behaviour', take a rest, take a day out. But start the next day.

No one will publish it, anyway.
Hang on, you haven't even started yet! Start writing.

Step 12: Bold first steps

Take it away!
Premise: there comes a point when we talk no more, we study no more, we plan no more – we start, we take action we do something. We get on the path to the success we want. That is the very essence of JfDI! So: JfDI! Just Do It.

Here are some big bold first steps:

- Write your main character.
- Write why your way of designing a new garden is so easy. Write the blurb for the back of the book.
- Write the www.amazon.co.uk synopsis for your book.
- Write the opening chapter for your book.
- Order the software up-grade for your word-processing software.
- Buy yourself a new lap-top.
- Buy a nice new fountain pen and plenty of cartridges.
- Join a creative writing group.
- Write a proposal for your non-fiction book and send it to 15 publishers.
- Take a first step.

Things to do

Step 1: Choose a brilliant, supporting mindset. How about, simply: 'I am a writer'?

Step 2: Create the most powerful VEMM ever. You, the writer at the lap-top. The words being produced. Being delighted with a chapter, a character, an explanation.

Step 3: What's the strategy you'll give most focus to? If you answered anything but write it was the wrong answer!

Step 4: What are the critical tactics? Start using them. Sitting down at the writing desk. Writing every day. These are great tactics.

Step 5: Are you inclined to act? Get so you are. Get enough sleep. Write at your best times.

Step 6: Have you worked your pain/pleasure lever? Are you clear about what's going to happen if this change doesn't happen?

Step 7: Have you broken it down, and broken it down. And dated it?

Step 8: Is it 'in yer face'?

Step 9: What's the high pay-off?

Step 10: What old patterns do you need to break?

Step 11: You know that only you can block you, don't you?

Step 12: Get to it!

NB's thoughts

This was an important desire for me. I had put it off for a while as I didn't feel I had an original angle that I wanted to pursue. And time with our young family was vital. However, as the ideas nurtured, the children got a little older and my teaching audiences were increasingly asking me for a book, it was time to put pen to paper and fingers to keyboard.

Discovering Julia Cameron's book The Artist's Way *came just at the correct time (as things often do). The encouragement just to write and to demystify the art was crucial. As with any skill, it takes time and practice.*

Desire 4: To achieve financial independence

As we have mentioned, desires 1 (To lose weight, get fit, feel well and attractive) and 2 (To stop smoking) often fall into the category of 'have to's' for an individual. Also as we discussed, desire 3 (writing a book) is perhaps a little different: no one has to write a book; it truly does come under the heading of wish or desire. Desire 4, to achieve financial independence, is an equally fascinating one.

So, what are we talking about here? We're talking about achieving a state whereby we do not need to work unless we wish to do so. We are literally independent of external finances.

How is this expressed?
- I'd love to feel I only worked because I wanted to.
- I'd love to have more financial freedom.
- I hate having to work so hard all of the time.
- I want to take a break from this and try something different, but money is an issue.

Step 1: Give ATTENTION at BRAIN level

Adjusting your mindset to support your change
Fundamental premise: mindset dictates behaviours which dictate results, so develop a supportive mindset.

Here are some excellent mindset statements to have if you wish to develop financial independence:
- *I recognise that financial independence is above all a mindset.* It is above all a decision to *disconnect* my life and many of its qualities from an over-dependence upon my financial situation. To begin to question whether many of the truly important aspects which I crave such as great relationships, freedom and time for me actually need much financial attention.

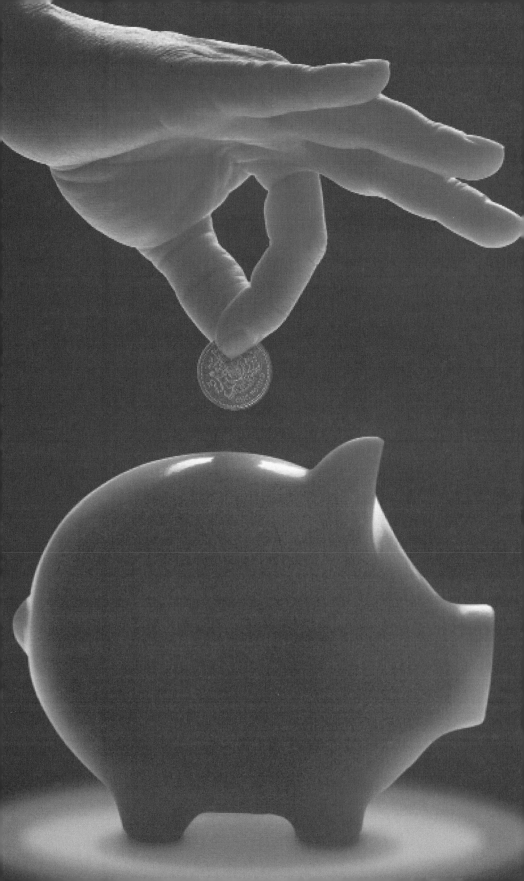

- *I recognise that a certain amount of money is crucial, obviously.* But perhaps that amount is actually smaller than I have been led to believe. Perhaps I have been seduced by the promise of a lifestyle. Perhaps I am still enamoured by a series of toys. And maybe if I am serious about financial independence I can decide not to be seduced by such messages and by the marketers.

- *I can improve my financial situation.* There is absolutely no doubt that you can. Many people's finances are in a dreadful state; perhaps they have never taken control since their student days. Perhaps the costs of bringing up a family have been surprisingly heavy. Perhaps lifestyle aspirations have spiralled (upwards!). For many others their finances are simply not optimised. And for a third set, they are not being as creative as they might. We'll address all three.

- *I understand why I want this.* Because independence will not be achieved or may be achieved at too high a cost without understanding this point. Why do you want it?

    - **Status.** After all, perhaps it would be cool if people around you realised you just worked because you enjoyed it and made decisions because of what you wanted to do rather than just 'the money'.
    - **Security.** The best form of security there is? After all, a quarter million or two million in the bank – whatever. You're going to feel secure, aren't you?
    - **To prove you can do it.** What a great goal, what a great challenge. And for a creative achiever such a yourself it should be very straightforward.
    - **Freedom.** The ability to take decisions with no one holding onto the purse-strings.

- *I realise that financial independence can be achieved in many ways and it is subtly different to becoming wealthy.* If you are seeking financial independence for what might be considered the best reason, freedom, then that is within your grasp. If you wish to be purely wealthy, for wealth's sake, that will probably require value-building skills to be developed, e.g.

    - stock market development.
    - buy-to-let skills.

And that is beyond our remit. Don't let that stop you going for it, though.

- *I can get to understand all the jargon.* There is a lot of jargon and unfortunately it tends to be most loved by financial advisers.
- *It's never too late to improve my finances.* Whatever your age, whatever your status, now would be a good time to improve your financial situation.

And here are some to get rid of:

- *The rich get richer and the poor get poorer.* This is not the time and place to debate whether that is true or not. The fact is that does not dictate how you will fare. Simply adjust your mindset and get to work.
- *I'll simply never become rich nor wealthy.* Again, the goal here is financial independence. And if you are confused on the subtle difference, don't worry. You soon won't be.
- *I don't have the mind for finances nor numbers.* Maybe not currently, but you'll soon learn. Not sure what we mean by 'balance sheet'? Well take all your assets (everything you own such as your house and the painting your granny left you), less all your liabilities (the mortgage, the car loan). Guess what, that's a balance sheet. Now you are learning.
- *Planning is boring: live life to the full now!* Couldn't agree more! The decision to do a bit of work on achieving financial independence does not label you as a boring person, nor does it mean you are committed to a dull life. It means you are committed to more options and more freedom.

Step 2: Give ATTENTION at EMOTION level

Getting passionate and creating a vivid, explicit, mental model
Premise: we must get engagement at heart and gut level as well as at brain and intellectual level. Here we create a vivid, explicit mental model.

Given that introduction, what do you want? And what does it look like? The creation of a vivid, explicit mental model is going to be as critical as ever. Because this is potentially a very confusing area of what we want, what society says we want. Our idle fantasies. Our real dreams and goals. We need to get clarity.

So, what do you want? As always, get it into the positive. Clear and bold. Write it now:

....
....
....
....

Have you got it very specific? The sums you think you need? Why you want them? The lifestyle you are looking for? What other detail could you add?

....
....
....
....

Now imagine you have that state of independence. What are you seeing? Get very detailed. Not just that you are seeing yourself writing bills without concern, but also whose bills are you paying? And what do you do day-to-day?

....
....
....
....

And what else are you seeing? What are you driving at the moment? Now, what are you hearing?

....
....
....
....

How are friends reacting to this news as it slowly gets around about your financial independence?

....

....

....

....

And what are you feeling?

....

....

....

....

Now pull it all together so that you have around 500 words of sensory-rich description detailing exactly your new life. It'll obviously be your description, but maybe it'll be something like this:

> I am financially independent. I have managed my finances sufficiently well, managed costs and chosen a lifestyle which I enjoy – particularly because it gives me the time I want but does not revolve around a lot of 'stuff'. I have broken the connection I did have with wanting to be wealthy, as I now think Why? And I'm not sure I can think of a good answer and also it was distracting me from something I could achieve: financial independence. It gives me a great feeling of freedom and I love it.
>
> Although I am financially independent I still work because I recognise that is an important part of my 'purpose': I enjoy it.

Step 3: Give ATTENTION at STRATEGIC level

Selecting strategies to guarantee success

Here is our ten-point Financial Independence Strategy (FIS). Go for ten out of ten, i.e. adopting all of the points.

1. *Understand what you are seeking. Understand exactly what you really want.* Financial independence is essentially about freedom. Freedom from financial concerns, financial worries. Freedom from every decision, every move, every breath being so tied to money. That's the higher level thinking we are working at here. It is not simply about accumulating incredible wealth. In fact it is not at all about accumulating incredible wealth, because many who do are still not truly 'financially independent'. They are still worried, concerned and driven by those money anxieties. No, this is more concerned with the business of creating freedom. Because most people who say they want to be wealthy, when you explore that option with them, find that what they actually want is the ability to run their own life. And that is a broader strategy, as we shall see. Are you disappointed? Did you really want to know how to create a quick million; you thought it would get you out of a hole? Sorry, I don't think so. What will get you out of the hole is thinking in a different way.

2. *Start early.* The earlier you start (17 is better than 25 and 37 is better than 44 and 57 is better than 66, but whatever, *start*), the easier it is:
   - To accumulate. It is easier to save £10 a month now than much larger compensating sums later, generally.
   - To use the power of compound interest. Money saved now will generate interest. Interest will be gained on that interest many times over if you start earlier.
   - To develop excellent habits. Once started, the saving habit does become ingrained and there is always the expectation that money will be saved. The greater the delay in beginning to save, the harder it becomes to save as it often requires a shift in lifestyle.
   - To reduce early life debt. Early on we often have debt because of studying and from property purchase. The more we reduce these debts earlier on, the sooner we will reduce them.

■ To learn the ideas of the financial world. The earlier you start talking to people, the earlier you understand the definite scams, the maybe's and finally, the simple truths of the financial world.

3. *Know how much you need: set some goals.* Setting a goal never guarantees that it will be achieved. But setting a goal does means that it is more likely to happen and with feedback and adjustment it probabably will happen. Set goals by:
   ■ Deciding the lifestyle you want. Do it by decade. Simply sketch the time line and put divisions every decade. Now think of your requirements and correlate it with your VEMM work.
   ■ Commitments you may have, especially to your parents and to your children. What requirement might they have on your finances?

4. *Create a personal balance sheet.* Use this as a fundamental measure of how you are progressing financially.

5. *Adopt the following basic strategy:* spend less than you earn and save the rest. You may need to:
   ■ Adapt your lifestyle. Perhaps your expectations are too much at this stage in your life. Remember society in general may be convincing you that you need more of this stuff; but perhaps you don't.
   ■ Start some simple record keeping.

6. *Become financially literate.* Get used to thinking: balance sheet, return on investment. Understand the jargon of pensions.

7. *Understand the psychology of money:*
   ■ Disconnect happiness from money. Money does not create happiness. It's what money buys that can help *support* your happiness. And once we realise that, there are often more creative ways to getting what we want. For example, freedom does not really come through owning a Ferrari. Freedom comes from making a personal decision.

- *Disconnect your identity* – i.e. who you are – from money and 'stuff'. You are not your car. You are not your handbag. You are not a 'better' person for drinking Pepsi. And once you make that decision it becomes easier to change one's lifestyle expectations.
- Understand the difference between 'standard of living' and 'quality of life'. The two are not equivalent and ironically as we chase standard of living then quality of life can come plummeting down.

8. *Increase money coming in by:*
   - Saving and gaining interest.
   - By getting everything that is yours (e.g. complete your tax return fully and properly).
   - Asking for a pay increase. But do this on the back of increasing your value. Read my book *Being the Best* on how to increase your personal value to the organisation.
   - Going for promotion.
   - Breaking connection between time and money. Change it to a direct connection between value and money.

9. *Lower costs by:*
   - Buying sensibly.
   - Reducing debt.
   - Getting and re-getting best mortgage possible.

10. *Manage your finances through a spreadsheet.*
    - As we mentioned above, if you don't know how to use one, get someone to show you. Create two:
    - Firstly: cash flow. What comes in, what goes out. Keep it running in the positive.
    - Secondly: balance sheet. What do you own and have? What do you owe? Take the latter from the former to create your balance sheet.
    - Invest some money getting all your figures checked by a qualified accountant or a trusted book-keeper if you feel your personal situation is quite complex.

But above all, decide to become truly financially independent by adjusting your mindset.

Step 4: Give ATTENTION at TACTICAL level

Getting tactical to ensure vision into action
Let's now get down to detail. Here are the strategy headings from above repeated, but now with the addition of tactical detail:

Understand what you want
We're going to get especially serious for a moment now and I do hope you will continue to participate. We need to get to the bottom of what this money issue is about. Take an A4 sheet of paper. Head it 'financial independence'. And start writing: I want financial independence because... And fill the page with your reasons and thoughts. Write continuously and without judgement. Just keep writing. Keep writing. And when you finally get to the bottom, turn over and summarise in one sentence.

Financial independence is important for me because...

Start early
The earlier you start, the easier it is:
To accumulate:
- Decide how much *now* you will save.
- Decide by how much you will increase that each year.
- Decide when you will open your account.
- Open the account now, anyway!
- Develop a habit such that when you earn more you save proportionally more.

To use the power of compound interest:
- Start a new notebook entitled 'making money'.
- Note how much *now* is in your savings account.
- Re-note every six months.
- Don't take any money out and notice the compound effect.

To develop excellent habits:

- Stop wasting money, e.g. plan your food shopping, mix designer clothes with some ordinary which no one would identify.

To reduce early life debt:

- Get rid of one credit card now.

To learn the ideas of the financial world:

- Buy one book on financial literacy appropriate to your knowledge level and start now.
- Find a financially literate buddy and get them to explain things in simple terms, e.g. pensions.

Know how much you need: set some goals

Setting a goal never guarantees that it will actually happen. But setting a goal means that it is more likely to happen and with feedback and adjustment it probably will happen. Set goals by:

- Deciding the lifestyle you want. Do it by phase. A time when you won't need to earn money but probably still active and travelling, etc.
  - A great way to do this is through a storyboard time-line. Create a cartoon strip of the expectations that you have at each stage. Student. Shared life. Growing commitments: house, car, holidays. Kids maybe? More commitments: school fees, etc. Early retirement, with what lifestyle?
- Commitments you may have, especially to your own parents and to your own children:
  - Write down any major financial commitments you can think of with an estimated amount. And ask whether that's really what you want to do. For example, many weddings can be a huge financial drain: is that what you want?
  - Get a qualified accountant to check your figures, to give some advice on how long-term figures such as pension projections will be changed as a result of inflation.

Create a personal balance sheet

Use this as a fundamental measure of how you are progressing financially. To calculate them:

Assets = house + car + furniture + paintings + cash

Liabilities = loans

Your balance sheet = assets – liabilities

Adopt the following basic strategy

Spend less than you earn and save the rest. You may need to adapt your lifestyle:

- Could you run a cheaper car?
- Do you need all the 'stuff' you continue to acquire?
- If you planned, could you reduce your shopping bill by 10%?
- If you have young children, could some of their clothes be second hand?
- Could you encourage more swapping of stuff; especially amongst children and their toys?

Become financially literate

Get used to thinking: balance sheet, return on investment. Understand the jargon of pensions.

Understand the psychology of money

- Disconnect happiness from money.
- Identify ways to have fun without money.
- Get used to reviewing what is actually great about life rather than constantly striving for more stuff.
- Educate your children from the earliest age so that they are not seduced into the consumer society.
- Disconnect identity from stuff.
- Decide that you do not want to be a walking 'designer label' show-room.
- Understand the difference between standard of living and quality of life.
- Have a conversation about the quality life which you are seeking and how you will achieve it.

Increase money coming in by:

- Saving and gaining interest.
- Getting everything that is yours (e.g. completing your tax return fully).
- Asking for and justifying a pay increase.
- Going for promotion.
- Breaking connection between time and money and substituting value and money.

Lower costs by
- Buying sensibly.
- Reducing debt.
- Getting and re-getting the best mortgage possible.

Manage your finances through a spreadsheet
- Get someone to show you how to use it.

Step 5: Create IMMERSION at BRAIN level

Getting resourceful

Premise: although many do give 'attention' to the change they seek, most then move on before the change is completed. We don't fall into that trap. We ensure we immerse ourselves in the change so that the change becomes irreversible.

We should at this stage have a strong inclination to act as we have already (1) created an empowered mindset to support us in this work (2) created a vivid and explicit mental model of what we are seeking (3) identified a strategy which will give us success (4) highlighted the tactics which are necessary to ensure the change happens.

We can reinforce that by:
Looking after ourselves: taking time out, getting sleep and getting data deprivation time.

By using the following affirmations:
- I am > my addiction to 'stuff'.
- I am > my fear of what the Jones might think when we start simplifying.
- I am > the label my spending power seems to imply.

When working on our financial situation we will typically initially be overwhelmed by the enormity of it. Therefore ensure you work on just one aspect of it at a time: just the cost reduction, just the savings plan, just doing the weekly shop more sensibly. One step at a time.

Step 6: Create IMMERSION at EMOTION level

Using the pain/pleasure lever

Working on financial independence is a good example of where we can be drawn into the detail and lose sight of what we were trying to do in the first place. The lever will remind us of this. It will keep us focused on the wood, even though we need to do plenty of work in the trees.

Q1: What will you gain by the change? Write quickly and without stopping. What is it that you will gain? What attracts you about finally getting in charge of your finances and on the road to financial independence? What attracts you about thinking about money in a very different way?

....

....

....

....

Come on, there's more to it than that. You won't just feel good about it. You will feel tremendous. Just imagine, not worrying about the credit card bills coming through the door. Knowing that you can make decisions for the right reasons, not solely because of whether you 'afford' it or not. Imagine your day not constantly revolving around price points.

....

....

....

....

Q2: Why haven't you changed? What pleasure do you get from where you are?

....
....
....
....

No – more honesty needed. Are you concerned about sitting down with that pile of paper-work? Or admit it, is there a bit of a rebel in you who really doesn't like to be too organised with such things? Is it too much of a sign of settling down and becoming boring and suburban? Or deep down are you concerned that this severing of ties from decisions being finance-bound is just a little too 'new-agey'?

....
....
....
....

Q3: What pain do you associate with making the change?

....
....
....
....

That's true. Is it also all that hassle with the various financial institutions and, admit it, you sort of like to wing it? Is it that you love money?

....
....
....
....

Q4: What will be the cost if you don't make the change? You need to get very explicit on this one. And on this particular desire, on this particular change: it really is a cost.

....

....

....

....

What exactly? And what would be the implications to your freedom and possibly to your old age? And possibly to your availability to support your dependents?

....

....

....

....

Come on, be honest, it's worse than that. What actually will happen if you don't make these changes? And what implications will that have for the future?

Step 7: Create IMMERSION at STRATEGIC level

Break and date
Now review your strategy. Review your pain/pleasure responses. Break your plans down into small, measurable actions. Actions which are brain- and time-friendly. And make them time and date specific. You'll decide yours. Here are some example ones:

Tony
■ I am going to work for 20 minutes every evening until I know the state of my finances; what comes in and what goes out. It's going to be painful, but I can cope with 20 minute chunks of time.

- I want to know my personal balance sheet by the end of this calendar month. I have a strong feeling by my quick calculation it's going to be negative.
- I've decided: no more holiday until I have cleared the £645 debt across my credit cards.
- At the weekend I'm going to get on the internet and renegotiate the car loan for a better one; the money I save will go straight against my credit card debt. I'm then going to get better at looking for the best deal on anything financial.
- But above all I'm going to break that addiction I have to spending and gross consumerism. I can do it. I gave up smoking last year, so I can certainly do this.

Frank
- I've been shocked by how much money I really earn per hour, i.e. when I took account of travel time and the long hours I work.
- I'm going to identify how I can break the link between earnings and time.
- I'm going to restore some of my life values: they seem to have got lost along the way.

Alison
- I need to get my business sorted: I'm spending too much time doing and not enough time planning.
- I'm going to calculate my personal balance sheet. I'm then going to project forward and decide my personal financial independence day.
- I want to return to the basic reason I got my business started: so that I could contribute. It wasn't so I could hit certain financial ratios for the bank manager.

Step 8: Create TACTICS at IMMERSION level

Commit to plan
Get your thoughts onto your wall planner: up on the wall and in every diary you need. Make it clear and bold. In particular ensure you schedule real time, i.e. financial planning 8pm-9pm not just financial planning 9pm.

Here are some tips:
- Ensure the planner is visible, not hidden in the back bedroom.
- Ensure you have both a big bold visible version and a portable one.
- Mark it with clear graphics and pictures.
- Importantly, celebrate successes with big ticks or smileys; whatever is your style.
- If you are in a buddy set-up: have rewards and celebrations but not counter to the hard work you are doing. E.g. don't celebrate reducing the annual mortgage by £365 with a drinking binge of £37!

Step 9: Create MOMENTUM at BRAIN level

Pareto power
What are the Pareto factors for your finances? Here we go:
- Really, really understand the true meaning of financial independence. Truly understand what we are getting at here. In this context, financial independence is the ability to run your life firstly with a mindset that your happiness, your identity and your primary purpose is not connected with money. Secondly money is simply a tool and that you will manage it wisely so that it gets back to being just that, something which worked for you, and your dependence upon it is minimised.
- You must understand that you are responsible for your long-tem financial independence. The government is not, your employer is not. You life partner is not. And if you are running your own business, the business is not. You are.
- You must understand the difference between these terms:
  - Standard of living and quality of life.
  - Spending and investing.
  - Cost management and go-with-the-flow.
- Financial independence is dependent upon you (1) starting (2) starting sooner than later.
- Finally, financial independence is not just about earning more, it is about (1) acceptance of appropriate lifestyle (2) enjoying what we have (3) simplifying.

Step 10: Create MOMENTUM at EMOTION level

Breaking the pattern

Here are 20 ways to do something radically different to start developing financial independence:

1. **Now:** decide that for the next four weeks you will reduce your alcohol consumption to just one quarter of what it is currently. For example, you will only drink wine at the week-end. The money you would have spent during the week will go in a jar (for dramatic effect) and at the end of the month you will bank the savings in your savings account.

2. **Now:** go on-line and find the best value savings account for you. Open it and transfer your savings and start earning interest. No savings yet? Open it with the minimum amount.

3. **Now:** take out any £2 coins you have in your pocket and put them in your savings jar. You will do that whenever you notice the jar. Every £10 or so you will buy the best book you can on managing your finances/understanding pensions/whatever, read it and implement the ideas.

4. **Now:** go through all of the kitchen cupboards and sort them out, so you know what you've got and don't keep buying extra bags of flour or new packets of cornflakes.

5. **Now:** look at your wardrobe of clothes and decide what additions you need. And which really need to be 'designer', but which could be bought more simply. And decide when you need these clothes: which can be delayed or even forgotten. Ask yourself, which is more important 'retail therapy' and/or 'financial independence'. And if the answer is the former, go back to the session on money and psychology.

6. **Now:** decide to have four days of observing your reactions to the world of consumerism. Are you seduced into buying things you don't really need? How are your 'wants' for clothes, for example, created? Have four days where you're in charge. Notice your choices: when buying, when choosing a coffee house, a cinema. Who's in charge? Decide that you will be.

7. **Now:** look around your book and CD collections and around the house in general and consider whether there is anything which could be sold on the internet to make a bit of money.

8. **Now:** do an analysis of your expenses: where does your money go? Could any of that expenditure be done more simply?

9. **Now:** create a standard shopping list and consider the best way to use it. On-line? Partly market, partly supermarket?

10. **Now:** have a discussion with your life partner about how you would like to manage your finances *for the best.*

11. **Now:** cut up one credit card, ideally the one which charges the highest interest.

12. **Now:** phone around for a better mortgage, but before shifting your mortgage, ask your own bank for a better deal.

13. **Now:** read chapter 1 of your new financial book. Or if you don't have it yet do ten minutes of learning from an on-line site such as www.motleyfool.co.uk.

14. **Now:** do a first pass on your balance sheet. How does it look? If it is negative what are the first things you could do to get it positive?

15. **How** much do you earn per hour? Now given the number of hours you *actually* invest in your work (including travel, working through lunch-time, continuing to work in the evening...), how much do you really earn per hour? Could you be earning that money any better anywhere else? What value could you offer?

16. **Now:** go back to your VEMM. How much do you need, by when and how can you start building it?

17. **Now:** less is more. Buy smaller, greater quality and enjoy them. Break away from the 'super-sizers'. Small chocolate bar, but the best chocolate. Small latte, but the best and enjoy it.

18. **Now:** network and find the best, most trustworthy financial adviser that you can. Ideally two so you can compare their recommendations.

19. **Now:**
    i.   How old are you?
    ii.   By when do you want to be financially independent?
    iii. How much do you need?
    iv.   What is your personal balance sheet now?
    v.   What will your personal balance sheet be at the age you gave in answer (ii)
    vi.   What is the difference between (iii) and (v)?

20. **Now:** how are you going to close the gap which was your answer to vi? Remember your keys are:
    i. change lifestyle expectations: don't down-grade, just simplify
    ii. save more now, more carefully
    iii. increase what you can earn per hour
    iv. get better return on all savings
    v. reduce all debt, earlier.

Step 11: Getting a STRATEGY at MOMENTUM level

Breaking through

Are you blocked? Are you unsure? Are you even confused? Let's stop that. Here are the top ten blockers to financial independence. And importantly, how to overcome them:

1. **Mindset:** 'it happens to others but not to me'. Pure limiting mindset. We're talking very simply here about getting your finances into control, developing an investment mindset and walking toward a new state of freedom. Step by step. Yes, it is possible.

2. **Lack of time.** You do have plenty of time. It's just what you put into that time. What you choose to do with that time. There are plenty of things which you know are a waste of time, or at best not the best way to use that time. For example, there is probably one TV programme you could not watch tomorrow night and it would not lower the quality of your life. And during that 30 minutes you could start work on this.

3. **It's boring.** Break the connection with all those figures which you hated at school. That's not managing your finances, that's arithmetic. Start and then you will find it interesting. What can be more interesting than learning how to make more money? Sex? OK, true. But you've got to agree, having financial freedom is still pretty interesting. And get this right and you'll have more time for sex.

4. **I can't understand it.** You won't until you get into it. It's like anything. Try describing how to ride a bicycle to someone. It's easier to get on with it.

5. **Who can I trust?** Yourself. Which is why you need to understand all the jargon. But having said that, you will begin to meet good advisers.

6. **I'm in such a mess, I'm trapped.** When you have a mess, when you have very little, it can be very debilitating. What do we do? Start at the very beginning, Make one decision on how something can be saved or a bit of money made. Maybe you could shop on a Saturday at the covered market for the vegetables for the first part of the week.

7. **I've built a pack of cards: commitments/kids, etc.** I do have money. That's been my problem, I have a lot of money, but I can't lay my hands on any of it. We have a lot of commitments, several houses... Ironically sometimes when we have so much, it can feel we have so little. Start again. With the basic questions. What do you want? How can you get there?

8. **My partner isn't interested.** He/she just says we have the money now so we should live now. Great attitude. But you'll probably find you are burning through money which doesn't need to be spent at such a rate. Simply make some sensible adjustments.

9. **Lack of energy.** No wonder your financial plans are in such a poor state: lack of energy can be very debilitating. Work on your state first.

10. **How do I know how much I need?** Agree your lifestyle. Simplify that lifestyle. Calculate how much you will need. How much do you now have? How can you close the gap?

Step 12: Bold first steps

Take it away!
So, what bold steps are you going to take?

How about, setting yourself the seven-day mental financial challenge:

Day 1: I will think how I can invest in me/us and not about how I can simply 'spend' our well-earned money.

Day 2: I'll consider how we can have more fun for free and equally brilliant holidays but at lower prices.

Day 3: I'll not super-size, but mini-size.

Day 4: I'll notice the seducers, and not be seduced.
Day 5: I'll ensure I am mentally financially independent, i.e. that happiness/motivation is not dependent upon money.
Day 6: I'll ensure our cost-base, without compromising what we really want in life is minimised.
Day 7: I'll review how I've done and set a date for another seven-day mental challenge in a month's time.

Or maybe decide that you will negotiate with someone – in a friendly positive way – to get a better deal, e.g. the bank manager, your boss, your mortgage holder, the guy you rent the garage from.

Or by thinking creatively I am going to end up with a savings jar with £5/£10/£15/£20 this week.

Or I am going to have the most detailed balance sheet and pie chart of where my spending goes.

Things to do

Step 1: Choose brilliant, supporting mindsets. What is the critical one for you? Perhaps independence is more important than wealth. Or I will not be seduced by the lifestyle merchants.
Step 2: Create the most powerful VEMM ever. Turn up the one you created earlier.
Step 3: What's the strategy you need give most focus to? Knowing where the money is going?
Step 4: What is the critical tactic: the saving habit?
Step 5: Are you inclined to act? Get so you are. Now.
Step 6: Have you worked your pain/pleasure lever? Are you clear in what's going to happen if this change doesn't happen?
Step 7: Have you broken it down, and broken it down. And dated it?
Step 8: Is it 'in yer face'?
Step 9: What's the high pay-off?
Step 10: How can you break that pattern?
Step 11: Have you accepted the only barrier to financial independence is you?
Step 12: Start

NB's thoughts

Society's expectations for you are high here. 'You're successful if you are earning more money', 'you are successful if you have more stuff' are the insistent, constant messages. 'You are successful if others are envious of you'. But how about if you were successful if you were enjoying your life and you'd managed to create one where your living expenses and running costs were low? So that allowed you to enjoy your life by giving you more choices. That would be pretty impressive, I agree.

Decide to live your life. Decide to create financial independence, but in a creative way.

Desire 5: To establish the career you want and/or the business of your dreams

This is a very exciting desire, something very close to the hearts and minds of many people. The two aspects are very closely connected, hence our reason for looking at them together. Establishing the career you truly want can often lead to you running your own business; and when you have the career you want you realise you are running our own business, even if it is for someone else.

Step 1: Give ATTENTION at BRAIN level

Adjusting your mindset to support your change
Fundamental premise: mindset dictates behaviours which dictate results, so develop a supportive mindset.

What are some mindsets which are helpful and supportive when we are working on our career, when we are working on our own business?

Achieving the career you seek
I can develop the career I want. You have a unique set of talents; that's your genetic asset. These talents need to be fully realised as they can become suppressed or stay hidden. You do that through your ability to make choices. And one of those choices is to find the work you love. That is not a naïve 'new age' expectation. As we shall see, it is a very practical career strategy.

I can find an appropriate use for my talents. Whatever your talent, from outstanding pancake-maker to photographer to counsellor, somebody somewhere needs and wants your talents.

As I use my talents I will enjoy my work. As I enjoy my work I will deliver of my best. As I deliver of my best I will be paid well. And that's why if your desire is to do the work of your dreams, you must follow that desire. And it will work out.

When I use my talents and enjoy my work I feel authentic. And this is a necessary state for human beings if they are to 'be happy'.

Business opportunity

There is a business niche which I can develop. You have an idea or ideas. They may be unique or they may be similar to someone else's, but you can develop a business.

My niche will be unique: maybe through product, maybe through service, maybe through my pure enthusiasm. Probably through a combination of all three. There is a mix that I can create: product + service + me which will be unique; after all there are so many permutations.

My offering will be best in niche. Because I am committed to excellence.

Step 2: Give ATTENTION at EMOTION level

Getting passionate and creating a vivid, explicit, mental model

Premise: we must get engagement at heart and gut level as well as at brain and intellectual level. Here we create a vivid, explicit mental model.

Given that introduction, what do you want to do? Or what do you want to create? And what does it look like? The creation of a vivid, explicit mental model is going to be as fundamental as ever.

So, what do you want? As always, get it into the positive. Clear and bold. Write it now:

....

....

....

....

Have you got it very specific? Does your new potential career have a job title? Or is it a 'career' you have created? What about the business you desire to start? Is it unique? Or is it similar to something else which is available (which isn't a problem – we simply need to know). What other details could you add? Where do you expect to work? Do you imagine this business becoming a large one?

....

....

....

....

Now imagine you have that career, be it an Ayurvedic doctor or a solicitor or running a stall at Camden Market or dealing in second-hand Morris Minors. Or maybe an holistic healer. Or imagine you have established your business, be it selling organic English wines or perhaps selling comedy show material to local radio stations.

What are you seeing? Get very detailed. And what do you do day-to-day? Who do you deal with? The general public? What kind of organisation are you in?

....

....

....

....

And what else are you seeing? What are you driving at the moment? Are you smartly dressed? Is it important?

Now, what are you hearing?

....

....

....

....

And what are you feeling?

....

....

....

....

Now pull it all together so that you have around 500 words of sensory-rich description detailing exactly your new life. It'll obviously be your description, but maybe it'll be something like this:

> I have changed my career so that I no longer work as an Account Manager in a large software company, but have got a job in a prestigious French restaurant to develop my career as a chef, which is my absolute passion. The money to be honest is absolutely dreadful but I don't need so much anyway, as a lot of my previous earnings had to go on 'compensation' activities because I was so miserable.

Or

> I have started my business which is an IT support company for small to medium sized businesses who do not have their own IT staff. This is of course not a unique proposition. What will be unique however is my pricing proposition which will be very very low, but asking for regular commitment so as to establish a regular cash-flow.

Step 3: Give ATTENTION at STRATEGIC level

Selecting strategies to guarantee success
Career you want
For the career that you want, our strategy is as follows:

Stage 1: Identify the career
To identify the career that you seek, you must be honest with yourself and discover what that deeper yearning is. This requires you to put aside

your limiting beliefs about what is possible and ask some fundamental questions which get you to explore what you really want to do.

You may well have achieved that in Step 2. In which case, excellent. If you are looking for some more help, then some follows now. Our basic premise is that you do in fact know what you want to do, it's giving it a little time to surface.

Ensure you have about 45 minutes of dedicated time for this exercise. Take pen and paper (or fingers and keyboard). Write quickly and without judgement, answering these questions as best you can:

- What do you want to do?
- Is that what you would do if money were no object?
- If there is difference between the two?
- Why is there a difference?
- Which aspects of your current work give you a real buzz?
- What do you love in your current work?
- What do you hate in your current work?
- What energises you?
- What do you want to do?
- Is that what you want to do, or what you think you ought to do?
- What are your first steps?
- What can help you?
- How will you get hold of that help?

Stage 2: Identify the opening
So, you know what you want to do. Try these questions:

- Where can you do it?
- Where are the openings?
- Do you need further qualifications?

Stage 3: The offer
- At this stage, write your proposal.
- Write your CV, your resumé.
- Capture what you are offering on one A4 sheet of paper.
- If there are courses to be done, start them now.

Stage 4: The chase
- Start applying now.
- Persist, persist, persist.
- Network. Ask people for contacts.
- Don't give up.

Stage 5: Deliver excellence
Now that this is your career, do an outstanding job.

Business opportunity
For starting your own business, our strategy is as follows:

Stage 1: Identify your proposition
- What business do you want to start?
- Why?
- What will be unique about it?
- Where will initial cash come from?
- Are your differentiators hard (quantitative) or soft (qualitative)?
- When will you start?
- How will you start?
- Who can give you help?
- Is it viable? Will you make profit? Will you have enough cash?

Stage 2: Create your plan
- You need a cash-flow projection.
- You need a profit and loss sheet.
- You need a marketing plan.
- Who can help you with these?

Stage 3: Deliver excellence
Never ever do anything less than your best: your business will thrive.

Step 4: Give ATTENTION at TACTICAL level

Getting tactical to ensure vision into action
Let's turn the above strategy into detail.

Career you want
For the career that you want, take our strategy and break it down into manageable tactics.

Stage 1: Identify the career
You did answer all of the questions, didn't you? All of them? Excellent. Now, leaving aside any ifs and buts for the moment, what do you want to do for your career? Come on, now. I said no ifs and buts. What do you want to do? And do you really want to do it? And is it a long/longer-term option do you think; by that I don't mean you have to do it for ever, but is it something which is more than just a whim? For example, many of us might fancy being a breakfast show DJ for a week, but it doesn't mean we see it as our career.

Excellent – so you know your dream career.

Stage 2: Identify the opening
Again, you did answer the questions, didn't you? So, you need to do some research. You need to get into the library. You need to get on-line. This career you want: where are the openings?

Stage 3: The offer
Write a brilliant CV. Include all relevant detail. Write a brilliant covering letter. Anticipate concerns that a future employer may have and pre-handle them in your letter.

Stage 4: The chase
Now give this massive attention. Really go for it. One stage at a time. Create the application letters, then get the interview, then get short-listed. Stage at a time. Stage at a time.

Stage 5: Deliver excellence
Now that this is your career, do an outstanding job.

Business opportunity
For starting your own business, our tactics are as follows:

Stage 1: Identify your proposition
- What business do you want to start?
  - Have you considered variations on that? For example, not just a 'coffee shop' but a 'bagel and coffee shop'.
  - When you have an idea see if you can 'twist' it to get an early differentiator compared to the competition.
- Why?
  - Status: proud to have done so?
  - Money: great revenue stream?
  - Love: change society?
- What will be unique about it?
  - 'Good coffee' is not enough.
  - 'Best carpentry' is not enough.
- Where will initial cash come from?
  - Bank?
  - You?
  - Friends?
- Are your differentiators hard (quantitative) or soft (qualitative)?
  - Hard = measurable and 'provable', for example 20% cheaper than the competition
  - Soft = more debatable, for example 'excellent service'
- When will you start?
- How will you start?
- Who can give you help?
- Is it viable?

Stage 2: Create your plan
- You need a cash-flow projection. Without cash even a viable business can die.
- You need a profit and loss sheet. Essentially, that's what you are there to make: profit.

- You need a marketing plan. It doesn't need to be too complicated. But commit a few things to paper such as:
    - Who are your customers?
    - How will you get to them?
    - Why will they buy from you?

Stage 3: Deliver excellence
Never ever do anything less than your best: your business will thrive.

Step 5: Create IMMERSION at BRAIN level

Getting resourceful
Premise: although many do give 'attention' to the change they seek, most then move on before the change is completed. We don't fall into that trap. We ensure we immerse ourselves in the change so that the change becomes irreversible.

We should at this stage have a strong inclination to act as we have already (1) created an empowered mindset to support us in this work (2) created a vivid and explicit mental model of what we are seeking (3) identified a strategy which will give us success (4) highlighted the tactics which are necessary to ensure the change happens.

We can reinforce that by:
Looking after ourselves: taking time out, getting sleep and getting data deprivation time.
Using the following affirmations:

- I am > concerns of career change.
- I am > fear of business start-up.

Step 6: Create IMMERSION at EMOTION level

Using the pain/pleasure lever
Once again, time for you to do some serious work. You need pen and paper or keyboard and screen. Here are your questions:

Q1: What will you gain by this change? Write quickly and without stopping. What is it that you will gain? What attracts you about changing your career/starting your own business?

....

....

....

Come on, there's more to it than that. You won't just feel good. It will be tremendous: managing your own destiny a lot more. Possibly better off financially? What else will you gain by this change?

....

....

....

....

Q2: Why haven't you changed before? What pleasure do you get from where you are?

....

....

....

....

No – more honesty needed. If you don't change, there's no chance of ridicule if you fail, is there? Is there status and a certain level of security to where you currently are? Will you need to let go of the BMW for a while?

....

....

....

....

Q3: What pain do you associate with making the change?

....
....
....
....

That's true. Are you even concerned about eventually revealing your plan to your current employer? Do you feel that they might make comments, such as you have let them down? Is there anything else?

....
....
....
....

Q4: What will be the cost if you don't make the change? You need to get very explicit on this one.

....
....
....
....

What exactly? What will happen to your sanity? I don't know how old you are, but how long do you want to stay with this 'if only' feeling?

....
....
....
....

Step 7: Create IMMERSION at STRATEGIC level

Break and date

Now review your strategy. Review your pain/pleasure responses. Break your plans down into small, measurable actions. Actions which are brain- and time-friendly. And make them time and date specific. You'll decide yours. Here are some example ones:

Jodie's actions
New career

- Read *What colour is your parachute?, 2004* by Richard Bolles.
- Read *Finding the work you love* by Laurence Boldt.
- Produce a brilliant CV: reference Jeffery Fox.
- Buy one-hour interview coaching including video play back.
- Ask everyone I know for honest feedback on my strengths and weaknesses, maximise the former. Start learning how to reduce the latter.
- Create some great speculative letters.

Juan's actions
Business start-up

- Create business plan.
- Visit bank manager.
- Write an initial sales letter and test it on some of my business colleagues.
- Sort out my personal finances in preparation for this change.
- Do some trial work in my three-week vacation to test the water.

Sue's actions
New career

- Take an extended break and think more fundamentally about what I want to do: do all the exercises in this section even though I normally skip such work.
- Read books by some of the industry figures who impress me.

Step 8: Create TACTICS at IMMERSION level

Commit to plan

Get it into your wall planner, up on the wall and in every diary you need. Make it clear and bold. In particular, ensure you schedule real time, i.e. 'sales letter work 7-7.30' not just 'letter 7'.

Here are some tips:
- Ensure the planner is visible, not hidden in the back bedroom.
- Ensure you have both a big bold visible version and a portable one.
- Mark it with clear graphics and pictures.
- Importantly, celebrate successes with big ticks or smileys; whatever is your style.

Step 9: Create MOMENTUM at BRAIN level

Pareto power

New career
- Ask the question: why do I want a new career?
- Get beyond a job title/label. What do I want to do? Who do I want to be?
- Establish what I like and what I don't like about where I am.
- Decide specifically what I want in my new role.
- Identify my strategy for doing that.

Business start-up
- Ask the question: why do I want to create a business?
- In particular, get beyond the 'making money' answer.
- What specifically is my idea?
- Why do I think it will work?

Step 10: Create MOMENTUM at EMOTION level

Breaking the pattern

Here are some pattern interrupts to help you:

New career

Set up some meetings with people who might be able to help:

- Those who have left your organisation recently and made good progress;
- A recruitment consultancy/head-hunter you feel you can work with.

Ask yourself: if I were really serious about getting this new career, what else would I be doing now to achieve it? And do it.

Business start-up

Set up meetings with those who can help:

- Those who have started their own businesses and made a success of it;
- Potential customers of your business; get some early feedback on what is important to them.

Do some initial sketches of your logo/letterhead.
Write your first sales brochure.
Reduce your personal expenditure by 25% for the next three months and put it into your business 'start-up' war chest.

Step 11: Getting a STRATEGY at MOMENTUM level

Breaking through

Let's take a look at the blockers you might face and let's handle them.

General

I simply don't have time.

You have the time for anything which is important to you. Make this important to you. Raise it in your consciousness. Get explicit. You will then have time for it.

I want to do it, but I feel waves of fear about letting go of 'security'.
There is no absolute security; being in corporate life, being in local
government, nowhere gives you absolute security. It is very important
to realise that. You have most security when you are managing your
own destiny; decide now to do that. You can do it when you are
managing your own company or when you are working for yourself –
it is a mindset, of course. Adopt that mindset now.

What happens if it fails?
It may well do so. But given your new-found inner security you will see
it simply as learning.

Start-up
I don't seem to be able to create enough uniqueness.
Remember it is very difficult to create true, long-term uniqueness.
True, original uniqueness is often rapidly eradicated by a competitor
copying you. No, uniqueness is at best a combination of you plus your
product plus your service. And while the product may be fixed, there
is a vast amount you can do to make the service and you even better.
For example, just imagine a more enthusiastic you.

No one will give me funding.
They will; keep trying. And if they won't, then maybe you need to
structure things in a different way.

Will people think we're too small to give serious business?
Not if you act in a professional way. Many people love dealing with
smaller companies because that is how they get much better attention.

Career change
Early reaction says that I simply don't have enough experience.
Keep trying. Maybe you need to take a side-step in your career, and
then re-approach.

Step 12: Bold first steps

Take it away!

It's time. No more procrastination, no further delays. Time to get on with it. Here are some suggested big, bold first steps:

Career change

■ Subscribe to the paper/journal which has most ads for the career you seek. Do it now.

■ Get some professional advice on your CV. Arrange it now.

■ Go to Ryman's and get some smart folders to enclose your CV. Go shopping now.

■ Go to town and get a new outfit for you interviews. Get you hair sorted. Arrange it now.

Business start-up

■ Pick up your mobile and make a call to someone who will be surprised by your plan and also how far developed it is, but will be supportive to you. Now!

■ Go and take a look at potential office space. Now!

■ Do a competitor day: get pricing lists and as much information as you can from/about your potential competitors. Now!

Things to do

Step 1: Choose brilliant, supporting mindsets. What is the critical one for you? Perhaps 'I will never be the real me until I follow this desire through to completion: I must have a go at running my own business or I must pursue this career interest.'

Step 2: Create the most powerful VEMM ever. Turn up the one you created earlier; even more detail, even more focus. What exactly are you doing with this change?

Step 3: What's the strategy you give most focus to? Possibly following that gnawing intuitive feeling you have about what you should be doing?

Step 4: What are the critical tactics?

Step 5: Are you inclined to act? Get so you are; stop being an arm-chair entrepreneur.

Step 6: Have you worked your pain/pleasure lever? Are you clear in what's going to happen if this change doesn't happen?

Step 7: Have you broken it down, and broken it down? And dated it? Do so.

Step 8: Is it 'in yer face'? Are these plans ever present? On your mind?

Step 9: What's the highest pay-off activity? That first visit to the bank manager?

Step 10: How can you break the pattern? Go on, do something now. You want to be a life coach, do your first ad – first three responses get a 45 minute session free.

Step 11: What's blocking you? Fear? Analyse it, get it in proportion: don't allow it to grow.

Step 12: Start. Go on. Put together your new CV.

NB's thoughts
Career
Changing the direction of your career is not an indication that you have made a mistake; it is a sign that you are growing. When we grow we do change our mind and we do change direction. Our career is so important to us; it is after all a primary source of our happiness. I have made several career changes to get to where I am now: you will no doubt do the same. After all, one of the continuing challenges with the school environment is that often little encouragement is given for potential career interests outside the mainstream and equally that an expectation is often implied that this is a 'choice for life'.

Your own business
Starting my own business was exhilarating, daunting: the full range of emotions. Strategic Edge started small, grew large and I've now deliberately made it small again, so that I am able to dedicate more time to my writing. If it's a desire of yours go for it. It will be one of the toughest things you will do. But it has to be said that it is no longer true that it offers you less security than being with a large corporation.

So, plan, prepare, do everything you can to increase your chances of success. And then go for it. Whatever happens, you are becoming more of an entrepreneur – and everyone wants that skill set.

Desire 6: To find and keep true love

Is it possible? To find true love? To keep true love? In a society where the statistics on divorce seem to get worse every time they are announced, when the length of time two people are willing to commit to each other seems to get shorter and shorter, when it seems harder and harder to find anyone who really wants to commit anything fully to a relationship, nearly every indicator appears to suggest it is not possible. And yet, and yet.

Of course we must all decide what we want for our relationship and what kind of relationship we want, but there is no doubt that true love can be found and that it can be maintained. If you want it to.

Step 1: Give ATTENTION at BRAIN level

Adjusting your mindset to support your change

As always, let's start with mindset. Because this will dictate the level of success you have. You must have a mindset which supports – in this most sensitive of areas – the behaviours you are seeking. Here are some suggested ones:

- *I can find someone to share my life.* Why not? Maybe it's been hard so far. Maybe you have been let down once or twice or more in the past. But that is no reason to stop believing you can find someone to share your life. There are a lot of people out there who want to share your life. The challenge you both have is making contact with each other.
- *There are many ideal people out there.* There is no one perfect person, because by definition they would need to change to accommodate you. But there are several 'perfect' people out there who can learn to live with and love you.
- *This is an opportunity to learn a lot about me.* On your quest to find the person of your dreams, if you are willing to learn more about yourself then it will both be easier and it will be fun.

- *I can re-invent this relationship.* I crave the 'old days' when we had time, fun, great sex. Silliness. Indeed. And with that in mind, re-invent your current relationship for now. After all, you are more mature, you may have a little more stability in your lives. That should only make it easier.

Here are some to get rid of:
- *I will never find the person of my dreams.* You will, you need the right approach. And that is what this section is about.
- *And if I do, it won't last.* A relationship can last, and we will look at approaches to ensure it does. Statistics are just statistics. They do not mean that your own particular relationship is doomed.

Step 2: Give ATTENTION at EMOTION level

Getting passionate and creating a vivid, explicit, mental model
Premise: we must get engagement at heart and gut level as well as at brain and intellectual level. Here we create a vivid, explicit mental model.

Given that introduction, what do you want? And what does it look like? The creation of a vivid, explicit mental model is going to be as critical as ever.

So, what do you want? As always, get it into the positive. Clear and bold. Focus either on the finding or the keeping, just for the moment. Write it now:

....

....

....

....

Have you got very specific? What will the person be like? What will your new improved relationship be like?

....

....

....

....

Now imagine you have that relationship you have been seeking. What are you seeing? Get very detailed. How are you spending time? And what do you do day-to-day?

....

....

....

....

And what else are you seeing? Now, what are you hearing?

....

....

....

....

What sort of conversations do you have? About what?

....

....

....

....

And what are you feeling?

....

....

....

....

Now pull it all together so that you have around 500 words of sensory rich description detailing exactly your new life. It'll obviously be your description, but maybe it'll be something like this:

> *I have at last, I think, found the person of my dreams. It's early days, but it feels so different. The controlling nature of many previous relationships is not there: my partner is relaxed about me seeing my old friends and doesn't ask me to give up my old way of life. I have new levels of energy, and feel a lot more 'whole'. I think that is a good sign. In previous relationships I have felt torn....*

> *We seem to have a common understanding of some future plans, and although we disagree on plenty, we do seem to be building a good respect for each other and a common set of values.*

OR

> *That's really what it needed: to realise that this relationship of ours after seven years has become a bit stale and possibly that's why I have been getting 'itchy feet'. But I can revitalise it. After all, underlying all the day-to-day hassle of long commutes and problems with money and local schools we have a brilliant relationship. I need to work on it. I need to give it some attention. And simply thinking like this is making me feel lot better about the whole thing.*

Step 3: Give ATTENTION at STRATEGIC level

Selecting strategies to guarantee success

There are two aspects to the strategy:

Firstly, finding true love:

Idea 1: Spend some time deciding: 'what do I want in my partner-for-life?'. Describe who they are as well as what they look like. Base your thinking on all of the relationships you have had: those that have worked and those that haven't. Consider the lifestyle you live now and expect to be living. How does that impact the relationship you are looking for? Your VEMM will have had this primary function: maybe go back to your VEMM and expand it even further.

Idea 2: Once you are making progress with describing the person you wish to spend more time with, think about where those people would spend time and join some of those events. The people you want to meet, what do they do, where do they go to? In essence, how can you mingle with more of those people?

Idea 3: Register on-line with various dating agencies. There are a plethora available now. Yes, I know you feel it is not a romantic way to find your future soul-mate. But let's be pragmatic: we need to find them; then we can be romantic! What's your favourite newspaper? They'll have contacts you can text straight away.

Idea 4: Network. Take every opportunity you can to find the person of your dreams. Don't turn down parties or dinner parties unless you truly hate them. And if you do, find an alternative way to network. Don't say you're shy. You're not shy with the 'right' people. Maybe you should join a week-end conservation group work-party. Come on, think laterally.

Idea 5: Stay open to possibilities, especially if you have been a bit disappointed that none of those ideas seem very romantic. You never know where a conversation might lead you. That person on the train who helped you with your luggage... And without getting yourself into dangerous situations, do occasionally be bold. So you had a nice conversation and the train has arrived at the main station, go on, ask him if he has time for a coffee. Otherwise you're only going to be spending the next month saying to yourself 'if only'.

Idea 6: Look after yourself. For two very good reasons. Firstly, we will be very much more attractive when we are well: we will feel loving/romantic/sexy. Secondly we will choose more balanced relationships when we are well: we will not be or feel desperate or fall into some of our old unhelpful patterns.

Idea 7: Once the relationship starts, enjoy the sex, the body chemistry. It's where the initial focus tends to be, of course. It's fantastic but also do a bit of talking. What makes your partner tick? Is this someone who could become a long-term friend, lover and life partner? Or is it just some short-term fun? Don't allow the short-term, very powerful chemical buzz to cloud the longer-term wish you may have.

Idea 8: Any relationship that doesn't work, ask yourself, what was wrong there? Was it them, or was it in fact you? Probably a bit of both, of course. When relationships don't work, consider:

- Recurring patterns: is there something you do, or something you seek which messes the relationship up? Can you change it or is it simply part of you and therefore you need to adjust the relationship?
- Possible feedback for you. Ask the power question: what does this say about me?

Idea 9: Not having any luck? Leave it for a while: you are trying too hard. Just when you are not looking, you'll find the right person.

Idea 10: Stay open-minded. Only one of these ideas has to work! And they will work, but you need to do the idea. Not just read it!

Secondly, keeping the person of your dreams. Here are ten ideas for keeping the person of your dreams:

Idea 1: Keep talking. Be interested and interesting. Never ever let your relationship become routine.

Idea 2: Keep dating. Get romantic time. Book week-ends, book meals. Go for a walk in the park. Talk as you used to talk. And talk more deeply that you were able when you first met because you didn't have time or you didn't want to trouble your partner with your concerns.

Idea 3: Discuss your beliefs, your values, your boundaries.

Idea 4: Learn stuff together, but grow separately too.

Idea 5: Support your partner's dreams. Don't cage them, free them.

Idea 6: Have your own time and your own interests. Nurture other friendships.

Idea 7: Get the logistics of a relationship – money, admin, responsibilities – sorted. Then relax!

Idea 8: Be loyal, be polite. Don't be rude about them to your friends.

Idea 9: Love them in their way; if they like to be left for a while to read, then respect that.

Idea 10: Stay young. They'll change. You need to, too.

Step 4: Give ATTENTION at TACTICAL level

Getting tactical to ensure vision into action

Finding your ideal partner

Idea 1: What do you want? Ask yourself:
- Who are they?
- What do they do?
- What is important to them?
- What are their values?

Idea 2: Where will they be?
- Where might you find them?
- What are their interests?

Idea 3: Register.
- Review your current reading matter: use that as a guide as to where to register on-line.

Idea 4: Network.
- Ask good friends for interesting contacts.
- Listen out for people you might like to meet.

Idea 5: Stay open to possibilities:
- Particularly day-to-day situations which get you into new situations.
- Notice any extra 'magic' in a simple interaction.

Idea 6: Look after yourself:
- Stay fit.
- Eat well.
- Invest in yourself: hair, nails, clothes (that's for you men, too).

Idea 7: Once started

Idea 8: Learn
- What does this say about me?

Idea 9: No luck?
- Take a break.

Idea 10: Stay open-minded
- Only one idea needs to work.

Keeping the person of your dreams

Idea 1: Be interested and interesting:
- Break routines: try different holidays, different restaurants and different Christmases.
- Keep talking, keep sharing.
- Argue and discuss, but with love.
- Read widely; swap books.
- Get out more: museums/art galleries.

Idea 2: Keep dating:
- Be proactive: have ideas and suggest them. Put time aside and in the diary.
- Do the extras with no reason at all. Flowers just for the sake of flowers.

Idea 3: Keep discussing:
- What do you really differ on? And accept those differences. That was why you fell in love, remember?
- What really bugs you about your partner's behaviour? And be prepared to accept criticism. Stay loving.

Idea 4: Learn:
- About yourself.
- To be a better partner.

Idea 5: Support:
- Your partner's ideas – maybe it is crazy to re-train as a doctor at age 42, but what the heck.

Idea 6: Have your own time:
- Take time out: own time, own friends, own interests.

Idea 7: Sort logistics:
- Agree your financial structure: who pays for what?
- Plan your finances.
- Work as a team: housework, parenting if relevant.

Idea 8: Be loyal and polite:
- Always be loyal.
- Always be polite.

Idea 9: Love them:
- For who they are, because they can't become your image.

Idea 10: Stay young at heart:
- Be flexible.
- Times change.
- You change.

Step 5: Create IMMERSION at BRAIN level

Getting resourceful

Premise: although many do give 'attention' to the change they seek, most then move on before the change is completed. We don't fall into that trap. We ensure we immerse ourselves in the change so that the change becomes irreversible.

We should at this stage have a strong inclination to act as we have already (1) created an empowered mindset to support us in this work (2) created a vivid and explicit mental model of what we are seeking (3) identified a strategy which will give us success (4) highlighted the tactics which are necessary to ensure the change happens.

We can reinforce that by:
- Looking after ourselves: taking time out, getting sleep and getting data deprivation time.
- Using the following affirmations:
    - I am > pulls in other directions.
    - I am > memory of poor relationships.
    - I am able to improve this current relationship.

Step 6: Create IMMERSION at EMOTION level

Using the pain/pleasure lever

Once again, time for you to do some serious work. You need pen and paper or keyboard and screen. Here are your questions:

Q1: What will you gain by this change? Write quickly and without stopping. What is it that you will gain? What attracts you about establishing a new relationship or improving your current one?

....

....

....

....

True, but what else? What impact will it have in other parts of your life? How will it make things easier? What are you missing through not having the relationship you desire at the moment? What is frustrating you about your current relationship?

....

....

....

....

Q2: Why haven't you changed? What pleasure do you get from where you are? Let's be direct; why haven't you tried to get a new relationship? What pleasure do you get from the 'staying at home'? What are you doing instead?

....

....

....

No – more honesty needed. Are you concerned that it'll take up a lot of time and distract you from your current important career? Or deep down do you feel that the current relationship cannot be improved; is that a limiting mindset by any chance?

....

....

....

....

Q3: What pain do you associate with making the change?

....

....

....

....

That's true. Do you think your friends will comment? After all, they all seem sorted.

....

....

....

....

Q4: What will be the cost if you don't make the change? You need to get very explicit with this one.

....

....

....

....

What exactly? How will you feel about yourself? And what about the longer term, into older age?

....

....

....

....

Step 7: Create IMMERSION at STRATEGIC level

Break and date

Now review your strategy. Review your pain/pleasure responses. Break your plans down into small, measurable actions. Actions which are brain- and time-friendly. And make them time and date specific. You'll decide yours. Here are some example ones:

Hamish's actions

Wanting to find a potential long-term partner

- Decide what relationship I want. I'm clear on what I don't want, but I do recognise I need to get clarity on what I do want.
- Decide what would be good routes. I do enjoy dinner parties, but they're a very slow way and to be honest if you realise it's not a 'goer' the evening can be a bit of a pain.
- So, perhaps try some speed-dating and on-line. So need to write and experiment with copy for my profile.
- Get some decent casual jackets. The T-shirts don't look so good any more.

Peter's actions

Wanting to improve his current relationship

- Decide to book time at the week-end. With two children it's difficult but we can make it happen.
- Decide to have at least one 'romantic candle-lit dinner' a fortnight. And I'll do the cooking!
- Decide to make a real fuss of special occasions; they tend to become subsumed by children stuff.

Anna's actions

Wanting to discover 'what do I want in a relationship?'

- Work on me first. I'm so stressed at work and always feel I need to 'do work'. I know I'm not fun to be with. Let's take a month out to work on me.
- Go on an assertiveness course to push back at work.
- When that's done, create some boundaries at work and re-evaluate what I really want out of a relationship.
- And for the moment, cancel all the 'dating club' stuff.
- In a month's time when I'm sorted, start again.

Step 8: Create TACTICS at IMMERSION level

Commit to plan

Get it into you wall planner, up on the wall and in every diary you need. Make it clear and bold. In particular ensure you schedule real time, i.e. write Sunday 1-10pm, our time.

Here are some tips:
- Ensure the planner is visible, not hidden in the back bedroom.
- Ensure you have both a big bold visible version and a portable one.
- Mark it with clear graphics and pictures. Ads placed. Replies done. Meetings planned.

Mark on it:
- Meetings
- Special occasions
- Slots to go birthday presents shopping
- Time to put aside to work on your latest 'on-line' ad.

Step 9: Create MOMENTUM at BRAIN level

Pareto power

What is the essence of what we really need to do here? It's actually incredibly simple. To find and keep true love we must think: quantity times quality.

For finding

Quantity: meet as many potential partners as you can.

Quality: be you, the real you, but be your 'best real you' at the meetings. Be interested. Be interesting.

For keeping

Quantity: get time together, even if you need to 'book' it. And if you are busy, if you are commuting and/or travelling a lot, if you have children, if you have a demanding career, you will probably need to do so.

Quality: when you are with your partner, be there, mentally and emotionally as well as physically.

Step 10: Create MOMENTUM at EMOTION level

Breaking the pattern

Get this change working for you by doing something radically different; go break an old pattern:

For finding

- Stop moping: get out with the girls/lads and talk ideas.
- Ring up an old flame up; go out. Talk and learn what worked there? Why didn't it finally work out?

For keeping

- Be outrageous. Spend £150 on a total makeover with the best consultant you can find. Look good, feel good. Stun your partner with the 'new you'.
- Think about some of the feedback you have been given over the years about how you act. Do something about it.

Step 11: Getting a STRATEGY at MOMENTUM level

Breaking through

For finding

- *Fear of commitment, getting it wrong.* 'I really don't want to get this wrong: so many of my friends have ended up in bad relationships and it seems to screw them up for so long. I really don't want that.' There is no commitment until you decide. Take each step one at a time. Enjoy each step and if you are not, stop.

- *Embarrassment:* 'I've never tried to find a new partner for my life like that.' Quite, that's the point. All you want is to find someone. Quite how you do it doesn't really matter, surely?
- *Time consuming.* Well, it will require some time. But do you want love friendship, passion, sex in your life? Or not? Or is your career the most important aspect of your life at the moment? If it is – so be it.
- *People will think I'm inadequate as I don't seem to be able to find anyone.* Everyone has challenges with their relationships. If they're commenting on yours it's only that they're impressed at how you persevere.

For keeping
- *If I change, my partner will be suspicious.* Perhaps initially, but not long-term as they begin to appreciate the stronger more enjoyable relationship.

Step 12: Bold first steps

Take it away!
It's time to take one. How about:

For finding
- Place that lonely hearts ad now.
- Ring them up and invite them out. You know you want to.
- Do something silly: leave a note on the wind-screen of their car.
- Mind-map what you truly want in your relationship.
- Talk to a trusted friend about how you might make progress.
- Read a recommended book about relationships.

For keeping
- Do something really nice for your partner even though it's not a special day. Don't mind when they say 'what are you up to?'
- Ring them up at work and ask how the day is going. Don't mind if they're a bit stressed. They will have appreciated it.

- *Listen* when they talk to you tonight rather than pretending to.
- Arrange a longer-term romantic week-end. Take a *really* cheap week-end break to somewhere beautiful. Florence? Venice? Go on.
- Arrange a shorter-term romantic week-end at home. Agree to cook two courses and do one each, to the surprise of the other. Be amazed when the two courses actually complement each other!

Things to do

Step 1: What's the critical mindset for you? How about: 'I can find the person of my dreams/I can make this a magical, long-term relationship. It's simply down to me.'

Step 2: Create a powerful 'visualisation'. What is this (new) relationship going to be like? Not just the magical, whirl-wind romance part but the day-to-day 'who's doing the shopping?' part.

Step 3: What's your strategy? How are you going to find him/her? Go for quantity.

Step 4: What are your critical tactics? Getting a make-over? Joining a dating club?

Step 5: Are you going to act? Or are you going to complain?

Step 6: Have you worked your pain/pleasure lever? Are you clear about what's going to happen if this change doesn't happen? Good!

Step 7: Break down the steps. You could write your introduction letter over several evenings. How about starting tonight?

Step 8: Is it 'in yer face'? Are you giving this the focus it needs? This relationship can be found, it can be improved.

Step 9: What's the high pay-off activity you can do? Do it!

Step 10: Go on, pattern interrupt. Place an ad in the lonely hearts! See what happens. Go on, plan a surprise romantic meal even though you normally forget your wedding anniversary!

Step 11: Start, do something now.

NB's thoughts

Finding *true love is a* quantity *game. Does that sound so
unromantic? But, it's true. That's why so many relationships
start at college or when we move to a new organisation
–where we meet so many new people. You've simply got to be
meeting people. And if you're not meeting the right people,
change your approach.* Keeping *true love is a* quality *game. It
is about putting time in to make it a great relationship. Your
partner will be different from you, that's why you chose
him/her and he/she you. But difference can become a pain.
That's when love is truly tested. Love has many aspects,
certainly one is physical love: lust. That's about body
chemistry; it's good fun and we shouldn't forget it. Love is
also about mental difference. That's the one we often need to
develop. Talk and walk. Walk and talk.*

*I know you'll find the person of your dreams and if you have
already I know you'll be well on the way to developing an
even better, stronger relationship.*

Desire 7: To be happy

Perhaps this is the ultimate human desire or wish. Perhaps it is the *only* desire or wish! To be happy! It is an ideal one for our final discussion; happiness is both the 'highest' desire in that it is perhaps the reason for many of the earlier desires that we have mentioned and developed and also it is the 'simplest' desire in that – as we shall see – much of the strategy for happiness is actually within us now.

So, what is it that you are looking for here? How do individuals often express this one?

I want to be happy.
I want to feel content and fulfilled.
I have so much, how come I don't feel happy?
What's stopping me being happy?
I just want to feel I have some purpose.
I don't want to feel so miserable.

As always, let us look at how to achieve our desire 'to be happy' through our twelve steps.

Step 1: Give ATTENTION at BRAIN level

Adjusting your mindset to support your change
Our fundamental premise: mindset drives action. Action creates results. So, for powerful change, ensure your mindset is supportive of the desire that you seek. A limiting mindset is our most troublesome and fundamental blocker. However, with awareness it can easily become an empowering mindset: our most powerful ally.

Here are some mindsets to adopt; perhaps some of them are yours already and you simply need to make them make more conscious so that you can fully benefit from them. Or perhaps some of your current ones just need a subtle 'edit' to make them more empowering. Whatever:

- *I can be happy.* This is fundamental. Whatever challenges I possess currently, whatever challenges I have had in the past, whatever challenges I anticipate, I know that I can be happy. Being happy is a complex mix of interacting inputs to my brain: physical, such as state of health, mental such as any current anxieties which we might have. But these are potentially much more under our control and management than we might initially suppose.

- *Happy for me is a state of contentment and optimism.* It doesn't mean I have to be always positive or always upbeat. I can allow myself to be 'down'. Happy for me is a fundamental part of my everyday way of thinking. Happiness is very much about being 'me'.

- *I accept that happiness is a choice.* Each day, every day, there will be challenges. Happiness is the choice I make at any particular point as to how I handle that situation. I can choose to be a victim. Or I can volunteer to make the best of the situation. Victim or volunteer: I choose.

- *I increasingly understand what happiness is for me, and increasingly understanding the cycle of happiness.* That I have a challenge, that it takes time to resolve. But I do resolve it and I feel 'happier' and then another concern comes along. As I recognise this rhythm – almost a spring/summer/autumn/winter rhythm – to my moods I am able to be 'happier' more of the time.

- *I recognise that long-term sustainable happiness* is less about what I have, less about what I do, but more about *who I am.*

- *I recognise that when things go wrong*, that needn't stop my happiness, it simply helps me on my happiness path by encouraging me to learn.

- *Happiness is my definition.* Not somebody else's.

Here are a few mindsets which are particularly unhelpful in the pursuit of happiness

- *This (my boyfriend ringing me/my winning the lottery/my getting this promotion/our having perfect weather on our wedding day/me being appreciated by the team for getting them that bonus) must happen for me to be happy.* Slowly, but surely, break the connections with things which apparently must happen (generally externally) for you to be happy.

- *I must own this (car/CD/shirt/pair of shoes/antique/bracelet) for me to be happy.* Be happy now: there's always something else on the acquisition path.
- *My partner must (enjoy parties as I do/want to go on personal development courses/enjoy family get-togethers) in my way for me to be happy.* No, you can be happy anyway. And you can be happy that your partner lives their own life, too.
- *I can only be happy when (I pass my test/I find the person of my dreams/I have left this job).* No, you can be happy at the potential of these things, too.

Step 2: Give ATTENTION at EMOTION level

Getting passionate and creating a vivid, explicit, mental model
Premise: we must get engagement at heart and gut level as well as at brain and intellectual level. Here we create a vivid, explicit mental model to ensure full engagement.

Let's ask our four 'power' vivid, explicit, mental model questions:

Firstly, what do you want? Spend a moment writing down your statement of what you want. You will by this stage be well versed in ensuring it is a positive, 'moving towards' statement. Start:

I want to be happy, which for me is

....

....

....

....

For example: I want to be happy which means that when I wake up in the morning... It also means that...

....

....

....

....

And now let's build our sensory rich image. You are now happy, according to your definition, above. What are you seeing?

....

....

....

....

Consider: how are you spending your time, what are you working on, what are you doing, who are you with? What does your day look like? What literally are you now seeing? What else are you seeing?

....

....

....

....

What are you hearing?
Consider: who do you talk with and what are they saying? And what are some of the conversations in your private life? And what other auditory input is there? Going to plays? Going to the cinema? Live bands?

....

....

....

....

Who are you listening to, what are they saying? What is important to you? With whom are are you having conversations? What are you feeling?

....

....

....

....

And where do you feel it? What brings peak feeling? What make you feel reflective?

....

....

....

....

Now review your writings and complete a paragraph which for you answers the question, what is happiness for you? And what does it look like, feel like and sound like?

....

....

....

....

You will of course have your description, but here's an example:

> I have decided to be happy. That is the key for me now. And I am increasingly breaking the connection with other things and people to 'make me happy'. It's an unreliable strategy and it's also expensive! In particular, although I love my mother dearly she is no longer going to have such a hold over my day-to-day happiness. Crikey! Some of those weekly calls would depress me for days. Hey, I'm not always 'up'. In fact there

are times when I am quite down, but the overall feeling is of positivity and progress. Life is good!

I've also made some clear decisions about where I want to live in London. I think I'd got such a hang-up about getting the 'right' area, it was really making me 'unhappy'. I've decided just to choose a couple of 'up-and-coming' areas and be more relaxed about the whole thing.

Step 3: Give ATTENTION at STRATEGIC level

Selecting strategies to guarantee success

Premise: for whatever we want there will be an approach, there will be a strategy. Our particular challenge is finding who has the strategy and does it give us the results we want? And is it the best strategy?

There are an abundance of apparent strategies for happiness. We will be discussing those which are:

- Sustainable, i.e. they are straightforward to maintain and do not require regular injections of 'buzz' to keep us happy.
- Self-referenced, i.e. they are ones which are more dependent upon what we do, how we behave and who we are and less dependent upon external factors, e.g. the weather being glorious or us winning the lottery. Such external factors are always a great bonus!
- Organic, i.e. they allow us to develop and grow.

Here are ten simple strategies that meet our four criteria:

1. *Decide to be happy.* At every point during the day, things can go well, things can go badly. We can decide to make a choice at any one of those opportunities and to be a possibility thinker, to decide what we can get out of this situation. Becoming a possibility thinker is to stay a 'realist'. It is not about being a naïve positive thinker. It is about saying, OK, I'm in this situation, how can I stay resourceful? By doing so, we maintain our happiness level.

2. *Decide to work on your mental and physical well-being.* We do not need to be in perfect shape! Trying to be in perfect shape could cause unhappiness. But as far as you can, invest in your brain and invest in your body. Eat well and read material which inspires. Whenever you feel down, invest in both: your body, e.g. go for a walk, plan some nutritious food; and in your mind, e.g. read a great book or go and see an up-lifting film. The state of your health, mental and physical, will determine a good deal of your happiness.

3. *Simplify, simplify.* Every day, every week, every month, every year, get rid of 'the crap'. Simplify your clutter, simplify your finances, simplify the way you travel, simplify the number of remote controls that you have around. Get rid of the fresh pasta-making machine which you never use. Chaos brings us down. We are simple creatures; we crave simplicity in these busy lives we live.

4. *Be here now.* Increasingly our lives are so busy that we constantly yearn for a time when things will be better. Stop. Be here now, just for five minutes. Reflect on what is going well in your life. Be happy now. And practise doing that more often. We used to have more rituals in our daily lives in all cultures, from the English 'elevenses' to the Japanese Tea Ceremony. These rituals engaged us with the moment. Create your own mini rituals during the day where you once again connect with you, your life and your happiness.

5. *Take responsibility for your life.* If you have been shirking this one, now is the time to take responsibility. This is your true coming of age, the one in which you allow yourself to manage your life fully. No one – the Prime Minster, your mother, the boss, Mrs Jones down the road – is going to decide your happiness. You decide it, whatever they do. Simply, stop blaming others.

6. *The big one: our career.* What we do to earn a living gives us a significant route to happiness. Because fundamentally it's how we express ourselves. So, work on your career. A lot more on this in a while.

7. *Be internally referenced.* Be wary of consumer pressure and external consumer seduction. Sure, if you're a huge fan of tennis and a big screen TV will enhance your pleasure in watching the game and you can afford it, then what the heck. But buy it because you want it and not because 'everyone else has one'.

8. *Be willing occasionally to defer gratification.* Sometimes it is well worth saving: that doesn't spoil enjoyment now, it certainly helps for the future and there is a tremendous feeling of inner strength and confidence which can come from being greater than the everyday pull which affects us.

9. *Flip-side problems.* There will be challenges every day. Flip-side them. What that means, is look at the situation in a different way. Decide that you will get the best out of whatever happens to you.

10. *Work on your personal development.* Invest in yourself. Develop your skills. Grow. Through growth comes significant happiness and contentment.

Step 4: Give ATTENTION at TACTICAL level

Getting tactical to ensure vision into action
Premise: nothing happens without attention to detail.

Let's take each of our strategies and see what you can do to get them up and running on a day-to-day, tactical basis:

1. *Decide to be happy.* To decide to be happy we need to be aware that we have a choice and that requires us to increase our self-awareness. Thus you are now aware of the fact that you are reading this piece of text, whereas perhaps just a few minutes ago you were simply just reading the text. How do we increase our self-awareness? There are three main routes:

   ■ Firstly, seek feedback on your behaviour at every opportunity. I agree many people are not good at giving feedback, but look for themes. If several people make the same point, then there is probably some truth in the matter. Through that feedback will come a great self-understanding and consequent greater self-awareness. At work, it will probably be scheduled anyway. But make sure it is given more than just 'lip-service'. In your personal life be willing to discuss with your partner how the relationship could be even better than it is at the moment and in particular how you could contribute to that.

   ■ Secondly, work on your personal development through reading and attending workshops. Clearly, the reading part you are doing already. Through fresh input to our brain and consideration of the ideas we learn more about ourselves. Good workshops, professionally run will significantly enhance that process.

■ And thirdly, take time out. By data deprivation. There are now so many ways that we can get input and input 24/7, that we cannot always get access to our own best ideas. Allow yourself some 'down-time' when you are not reading, not watching TV, not listening to the radio nor music.

2. *Decide to work on your physical and mental well-being.* As this was desire 1, you may well have done or be doing a considerable amount of work on this already. If not, I encourage you to raise its priority on your route to happiness. The simplest and most sustainable strategy is MEDS. This four-letter mnemonic reminds us of the four levels for physical and mental well-being: Mediation or taking time out. Exercise or developing our cardiovascular capability. Diet or choosing fuel for energy and great state. Sleep or ensuring we do not have sleep debt. To do more work on this, take a look at Desire 1.

3. *Simplify.* Each month, take a different aspect of your life and do a few things to simplify. E.g. month 1, take a look at your finances and get rid of some of the credit cards which have built up over time. Month 2, clear out the garage or the attic. Such activities are very therapeutic and allow us to focus on what is most important.

4. *Be here now.* Deliberately slow down. Notice the rate at which you walk and talk and get a coffee from the machine at work and eat your food at your desk and... Slow down a little: to a speed in which you are engaging with the day and fully enjoying it rather than allowing it to rush by and hurtling on to the next set of quarterly figures.

5. *Take responsibility.* Decide to own what happens to you. Decide to use the term I/we more often and 'they ' less often. When things impact your happiness consider what you might have done differently to handle that situation. Ask the question: what does this situation say about me?

6. *Work on your career.* Research increasingly shows that there are two main types of happiness: firstly, 'blip' happiness. That's a great film, a chocolate bar, much sex even. These blips of happiness are short-

term and are generally non-accumulative, i.e. they don't make us any 'happier' overall each time we do it. On the other hand, our career is a major source of growth for us and a chance for the 'artist' to be released and consequently for us to develop our happiness. And if you think 'release the artist in you' sounds a little grand, then reconsider. You are what you do. It's therefore important to choose something which develops who are and who you want be. You're an artist. It's just your particular magic might be baking or customer service or parenting, rather than oil on canvas or poetry. But if the artist is quashed, so is your happiness.

7. *Internally referenced.* Decide that as far as possible your happiness will be dictated by you rather than external events and issues beyond your control. Experiment with not using 'they' without an element of 'I'.

8. *Defer gratification.* Practise deferring gratification for the longer-term benefit. Your kitchen is fine; it doesn't need to be up-dated for another year: put the money into reducing the mortgage, first, which long term will give you more freedom, exactly the 'happiness' you have been craving.

9. *Flip-sided.* When things don't go to plan, practise looking at things in another way. So you are bed-bound with flu. Flip-side it: at least it's nothing worse, at least it's a chance to think, at least you weren't caught up in the traffic. You've been made redundant. Flip-side it: it's a chance to review your career, it's an opportunity to spend a little more time with the family, it's a trigger to finally get the finances under control.

10. *Personal development.* Consider the following topics for your personal development:
    - Your health
    - Your skill set
    - Your creativity
    - Who you really are and
    - What you really want to do.

But recognise that one of the most powerful ways of self-development is to help others. Whether it's a colleague who is new to your company and is unsure of how to get his expenses processed and one sixty-second tip from you saves him over an hour or an elderly gentleman struggling to get his shopping to his car to whom you offer help.

Step 5: Create IMMERSION at BRAIN level

Getting resourceful

We're making great progress, but how do we get immersed in this stuff? How do we ensure that it's something we *live and breath*? That we go beyond the *technique*?

Our *inclination to act* is our inclination to do something about our happiness. It is moving beyond *knowing* what we need to do to *doing* what we need to do. What will give us an inclination to act?

- A clear VEMM: we have addressed that.
- An excellent state: we are addressing that via MEDS.

Use these simple affirmations:
- I am willing to defer the short term for the longer term.
- I am greater than my day-to-day addictions.
- I will practise choosing happiness.

Step 6: Create IMMERSION at EMOTION level

Using the pain/pleasure lever

Once again, time for you to do some serious work. We're stepping on the accelerator now. You want this change: you want to be happier. Let's get it as quickly as we can. You need pen and paper or keyboard and screen. Here are your questions:

Q1: What will you gain by this change? Write or type quickly and without stopping. What is it that you will gain? What attracts you about being happier? Yes, it seems like an obvious question, but what does specifically attract you? What will it mean for you?

....

....

....

....

Come on, there's more than that. You won't just feel good. You'll have more fun and things will get done. And you won't feel so stressed. So what else attracts you?

....

....

....

....

Q2: Why haven't you changed so far? What pleasure do you get from where you are? Yes you do, otherwise you wouldn't be there. Be honest, it's sometimes enjoyable being a martyr, isn't it? Or at the very least you get a certain level of attention when you're miserable, don't you?

....

....

....

....

No – more honesty needed! Come on. Perversely, there's an odd kind of pleasure in feeling sorry for yourself, isn't there?

....

....

....

....

Q3: What pain do you associate with making the change?

....

....

....

....

That's true, but are you concerned about some of what your great but
more cynical friends might say: that you've become more 'positive'.
That you've become a bit 'New Agey'. And you know you'd love to go
on one of those 'heavy' personal development courses, but then your
friends would really think you had flipped, wouldn't they?

....

....

....

....

Q4: What will be the cost if you don't make the change? You need to
get very explicit about this one.

....

....

....

....

What exactly? What will happen to your health? To your feelings about
yourself? It's not so good, is it? After all, you have a long life ahead.
What's it looking like?

....

....

....

....

Step 7: Create IMMERSION at STRATEGIC level

Break and date

Now review your strategy. Review your pain/pleasure responses. Break your plans down into small, measurable actions. Actions which are brain- and time-friendly. And make them time and date specific. You'll decide yours. Here are some example ones just so that you can see the process.

Terry's actions:

- Decide to be happy.
- Flip-side anything adverse which happens to me.
- Work on health:
    - Take a walk every day
    - Go swimming at the week-end.
- Re-build my relationship with the kids which is causing me a lot of misery at the moment; that statement 'what does this say about me?' really rang true.
- Start reading again and intersperse that with some inspirational literature.

Sally's actions:

- Decide to be happy.
- When someone upsets me, ask myself 'what does this say about me?'
- Work on my physical state: walk taller, smile more.
- Work on career: appreciate it. I do enjoy it, but I've become so negative about it.
- Find a part-time job helping others: I really enjoy that.

Lucy's actions:

- Decide to be happy.
- Flip-side anything adverse which happens to me.
- Work on my career to change it. I've given it three years since college and it's not for me.
- Ditch the current relationship I'm in: it's controlling and just bringing me down. I've given it long enough.
- Create time to get back to my painting by reducing TV-watching time.

What are some of the factors which need to happen in your strategy for fulfilment and happiness? You want to move house? Sort out the guest room so that it becomes your painting studio? You want to save some money so you can go on that cookery course? Whatever, you need to break it down. Break it down so that the components are smaller, they are brain- and time-friendly.

Right, done yours yet? Come on then! Start writing. Break and break and date.

Step 8: Create TACTICS at IMMERSION level

Commit to plan
Now that you've got your list of actions, get them onto your wall planner, up on the wall and in every diary you use. Make it clear and bold. In particular ensure you schedule real time, i.e. career development 6pm-7pm not just career development 6pm.

Here are some tips:
- Ensure the planner is visible, not hidden in the back bedroom.
- Ensure you have both a big bold visible version and a portable one.
- Mark it with clear graphics and pictures.

Step 9: Create MOMENTUM at BRAIN level

Pareto power
What are the high pay-off factors in becoming happy? There are five:
1. Mindset: (a) possibility thinking (b) acceptance. Adjust your mindset so that it is 'happiness compatible'. By 'happiness compatible' we mean that we realise things don't always go to plan and therefore we are able to look at the possibilities which surround those situations. The second aspect of our mindset is to realise that there are some situations which are worth accepting, e.g. we will get older. And that is fine.

2. True affluence. Happiness is easier with the best health we can get.
3. 'Hygiene' factors. There are some basics which no doubt we need to sort out; so-called 'hygiene' factors. We hate our flat: it's dark and it's dingy. OK, there is a better one elsewhere: find it.
4. Purpose: career. Get a career which gives you a buzz, which gives you passion.
5. Growth and goal setting. Set a few goals. Things that you would like to happen. Notice that they do start happening. Notice how you feel about that.

Step 10: Create MOMENTUM at EMOTION level

Breaking the pattern

Presumably if your desire is to be more happy, then that is because you are not happy or as happy as you would like at the moment. As we have seen, one of the challenges of getting the change we desire is to break the old conditioning of the old state we were in. This is particular true when this state is as powerful as an emotion. So pattern breaking is very useful here.

Her are some questions to ask yourself:
- What causes unhappiness for you?
- With what do you associate unhappiness?
- Are there any things which positively get you out of the unhappiness state?

As you identify the answers to these questions, some answers will be minor and some will be major. Thus; in answer to *what causes unhappiness?* you may have put: the traffic, the demands of my boss, the fact that our youngest daughter doesn't enjoy school.

With what do you associate unhappiness? Perhaps, exhausting days at work. Talking to my daughter on the way home from school when she is upset.

What gets me out of that unhappiness state? Long conversations with my partner: realising and putting things in proportion. The week-ends with my daughter and realising that she does bounce back pretty quickly.

Tackle practically what you can. Thus it may well be possible that there is a more creative route you can take to work. Is there another school you could consider for your daughter, even if it would take a lot of fighting to get her there?

But what about those areas which seem to be out of your reach? Think out of the box, think creatively. Perhaps you realise that developing your assertiveness skills would really develop your potential, but your company won't send you on one. Well, perhaps decide not to go on your skiing trip this year but spend the money firstly on a highly recommended assertiveness course and secondly on four one-hour coaching sessions. The skiing is a one-off and you can do it another time. But your skills development such as assertiveness will last a life-time.

Step 11: Getting a STRATEGY at MOMENTUM level

Breaking through

What are the blockers to your happiness? As always, some of them are old favourites with any change and some of them are specific to this desire.

Fear. How can one be fearful of happiness? *It's possible.* We humans can be fearful of anything! To embrace happiness as a way of life has a lot of implications:
- Things might become 'too good'.
- Losing some 'friends' who don't like the new you.
- Realising that it is a choice and there is no one out there to blame but yourself.

Don't fear happiness, simply be happy.

Not deserving. Happiness is such an amazing thing. How can I deserve it when there's so much going wrong in my life?
- *Happiness is not a prize:* it is a state for living; it is an evolutionary motivator; it is a spiritual guide. We are designed to be happy.

History. How can I be happy? So much bad stuff has happened to me. *Maybe, but it is all history.* That is not to be unsympathetic. But it is all history. What can you take from it? What is the learning, that you can use?
■ The past does not dictate the future.
■ The past is history. You can design the future.

Acquisition. There is something I need before I can be fully happy. *There usually is.* We will be happier when we have got a bigger house. A bigger house in the country. And what you find is that there is usually just one more thing that we need. Stop it. Apart from the basics of life – the so-called 'hygiene factors', i.e. the roof over our head – 'stuff' in itself does not make us happy. In fact stuff can make us unhappy because it distracts us and we fall into the 'keeping up with the Jones' trap.

Insurmountable problem. *Every one of us has an insurmountable problem.* To us they can seem to be insurmountable: ill-health, stress, financial difficulties. But we will be best able to focus on these when we are happy. Does that seem crazy? Does that seem unsympathetic? The important point is that we can always find a reason not to be happy, because life's not perfect generally. Certainly not if it is real, if it is exciting, if we are growing. The reason we are in debt is because our start-up business is growing fast. The reason we are stressed is we have a young family and 'boy' are they demanding . But also they give us some of the most magical of times... Would we really when we stop for a moment actually want it any other kind of way?

Emotions. We can't be happy because other strong emotions are getting in the way such as the sadness/worry rollercoaster. When you are happy don't expect to get rid of other emotions. *We need other emotions.* Why?
■ To give us contrast: how would we know happy if we didn't know sad?
■ To give us information to stay on path with happiness. Sadness says: time to reflect. Depression says something is not right here. All of these emotions are tremendously helpful in getting back on path for happiness.

I don't know how to be happy. You do, otherwise why would you want to be happy?

I worry that things may go wrong. *They may;* accept that you can plan for a lot but you cannot anticipate everything.

Step 12: Bold first steps

Take it away!

What are your initial bold steps on this new path to happiness or simply greater happiness? They are so varied. They depend so much on you, your situation. But here are some ideas:

- Do something. Having reached this point you have put in so much work; will you do anything now? Of course. A good 'do something' is also something different. If you would not normally take a walk in the park because you feel you are too busy, then perhaps try that. If you might normally ignore someone who would need help, then help them.
- Start your thinking in a different way. How about giving yourself a ten-day challenge. Over the next ten days you will simply focus on what is working well, whatever happens. You'll put aside unnecessary negative thoughts and see how great you feel.
- Give more respect to your physiology and mental well-being. Remember they are delicate, they need looking after and you can manage to do that.
- Start work on some of these ideas with a good friend. Or maybe someone who isn't yet a good friend but as a consequence of working on these ideas may well become a good friend.
- Announce a few specific happiness goals. To yourself, to your friend, to your partner. To anyone who will be supportive.

Things to do

Step 1: Decide to be happy. Not ridiculously 'positive' all the time, just to notice what is working for you. Take on board the most powerful mindset you are able: 'I can be happy'.

Step 2: Create the most powerful VEMM ever of your version of happiness. 'Turn up' the one you created earlier; make it bigger, brighter, bolder. Increasingly notice how you are living that VEMM.

Step 3: What aspects of the happiness strategy do you need to most focus on? Your essential health? Simplifying your life?

Step 4: What is the critical tactic for you? Choosing your response? Just getting out a bit more?

Step 5: Are you inclined to act? Are you inclined to do something about this? Or are you going to stay stressed, stay miserable? Get so you are positively inclined.

Step 6: Have you worked your pain/pleasure power questions? Are you clear in your mind what's going to happen if this change doesn't happen? Really clear?! Good.

Step 7: Have you broken down what needs to be done and broken it down again. And again if necessary? And dated it?

Step 8: Is it 'in yer face'? How can you forget happiness, you say? Easy. And perhaps you have recently.

Step 9: What's the high pay-off action? For you? To decide?

Step 10: What's the pattern interrupt? How about a ten-day challenge? Focus on what might work well for you.

Step 11: What's blocking you? Nothing really, is there? It's not really time dependent or money dependent. Because so much of it is literally in the head. Only you can really stop a dramatic improvement in your levels of happiness.

Step 12: What step can you take? Do it now.

NB's thoughts

The breakthrough for me was realising that happiness is not dependent upon 'stuff', beyond a certain level. Sure it's critical to get a roof over our heads and a warm room for the kids to live in. It's brilliant to have the latest CDs. But there can equally easily come a point where the more we chase for stuff, the less happy we are. Chase time, health, relationships and career. Time to allow us to be happy. Health to allow us to feel good. Relationships to allow us to express ourselves. And career to allow us to be who we really want to be.

The second was realising it does not need to be dependent upon day-to-day external factors. It is obviously fantastic when the weather is superb, your stock price rises and the play you went to see was a delight. But treat ordinary days as days for being happy too.

Good luck with your quest for happiness. You are well on the path already.

Chapter 5
JfDI!: to go!

Introduction

You now know how to create any personal change you desire. You understand the three *phases* of personal change: Attention, Immersion and Momentum (AIM). You understand that for each phase we must work at the four levels, i.e. at Brain level, the logical analytical level; at Emotional level, i.e. what we feel in our heart, what we feel our gut; at Strategic level, what is our grand approach, and of course at Tactical level, i.e. what we will actually do on a daily basis. That gives us our 12 steps which we have applied in detail to seven case studies. So, you're pretty experienced now!

Remember that if you are not getting the success you desire either as fully or as quickly as you wish, return to each of the 12 steps and check that you are doing it *fully* and with *integrity*. Let's now do a final rapid review of the 12 steps so that you have a summary list, and now that you are an advanced student, let's focus on the particular *subtleties* of each step. This may well be a list you want to transfer to your personal notebook. Do learn it.

JfDI!: to go!

Step 1: *Give attention at brain level:* create a supporting mindset. Have any limiting mindsets begun to sneak in: 'this works for everyone else, but it won't work for me', 'how can I write a book if I can't get total peace and quiet?'? Put these limiting mindsets aside and return to your empowering mindsets. See both our general list and also the specific (per desire lists). No change will occur unless you have a supporting mindset. If you are working on change at organisational level or on cultural change, then recognise this must be a significant piece of your starting work, i.e. working on the mindsets of the individuals in the culture.

DO: use empowering mindsets.
DON'T: allow limiting mindsets.

Step 2: *Give attention at emotion level:* create a VEMM. If there is one area I find that people are often willing to skip, it's working on their VEMM. Those funny questions: it feels a bit strange! Guess what, that's the point! Feeling a bit strange answering them is getting you to think in a different way, a way which may well be the route to getting you the desire you seek. So, please do it. And if you're working at a corporate level you may find this a particularly challenging area in which to encourage others – until they start noticing the powerful results!

DO: create an amazing, powerful VEMM.
DON'T: ridicule the VEMM process.

Step 3: Give *attention at strategic* level: discover/create an 'excellence strategy'. Everything we do has a strategy: even being grumpy needs a strategy! Work hard at finding the right strategy, then the process of change will be easy. Some people work very hard with a poor strategy. That's frustrating! Is there one more person you could ask, one more call you could make, one more search on the internet to get that excellence strategy? And is there one more question you could ask of the person who is good at executing that strategy about how they do it and focus on the subtleties that make the difference for them?

DO: hunt down the best strategy.
DON'T: accept second best.

Step 4: *Give attention at tactical level*: turn your strategy into tactics. Yep, it's all very well knowing that to lose weight you must eat less, or to gain independence you must manage your money. But how do you do that if you are locked into the old pattern? That's what tactics are about. Ask yourself, what are the details? And are they concrete enough to follow? Has it moved from conceptual to reality so that I know exactly what I have to do?

DO: know what you need to do on a step-by-step basis.
DON'T: accept generalisations.

Step 5: *Create immersion at brain level*: check your state is inclined to action. You must ensure your state is one of inclination to act. And this is dependent upon you. Your state need not be dependent upon the weather, the state of your bank account. It is dependent upon the choices you make. Ensure as you work on your personal change that you are always in 'a peak state', that you *want* to tackle the issue. If you always work on it when you are in a peak state then you ensure that you will create a positive association with the work and you will find it even easier to do.

DO: get into 'peak state'.
DON'T: ignore that which seems obvious.

Step 6: *Create immersion at emotion level.* We need to get very clear about what drives us, given that all such change is driven by the combination of pain and pleasure. What is behind our thinking? Get absolutely behind what drives us. Ask yourself these most fundamental and prying of questions. What will you gain, what will you lose? What keeps you here? Why haven't you made the change?

DO: understand your personal pain/pleasure profile.
DON'T: skip this part and/or accept the superficial response.

Step 7: *Create immersion at strategic level*: date and break. Ensure that everything you have to do is both time- and brain-friendly. All of it. The human brain works best with a certain window of comprehension.

DO: break and break and break and break and date, until it happens.
DON'T: leave it unapproachable – it'll put you off.

Step 8: *Create tactics at immersion level*: schedule. Get it visible on the wall planner, in your diary so that it is always 'in yer face'. When stuff which we want to do is 'in yer face' it gets done. When it isn't, all kinds of stuff crowds it out. This is one of the simplest of the steps to action and it is often forgotten.

DO: get a great diary and wall planner. And use them.
DON'T: worry about becoming a control-freak and losing your spontaneity. You won't.

Step 9: *Create momentum at brain level*: the Pareto principle. The brain can only focus on so much at one time. That could be high pay-off stuff or it could be trivia. Ensure it is the former. Pareto will enable the brain to give maximum attention and get the change that is required. Be aware of trying to do too much, of trying to cover every angle of your health, of overly developing the plot for your book. Get on with it. Get on with that which will give you a high return.

DO: focus on the high pay-off to get your desire to happen.
DON'T: get caught up in time-wasting and debilitating trivia.

Step 10: *Create momentum at emotion level.* One of the most radical of the steps is literally that: to be radical. To say to yourself I am simply not going to allow this pattern to go around one more time. It's got to stop. Literally break the neural conditioning. Literally break the condition at muscle memory level.

DO: do something different.
DON'T: be overly sympathetic to your inability to change.

Step 11: *Getting a strategy at momentum level.* What are those final blockers? Some old favourites about 'no time'. Some new ones: 'can't find the strategy I need'.

DO: detail your specific blockers and eliminate them one by one.
DON'T: be seduced by new exciting stuff; you must eliminate those old blockers.

Step 12: *Create momentum at tactical level.* Take a step. And another step. Get on with it. And get on with it now.
Hey, you're all set!

DO: do it.
DON'T: stop now.

Chapter 6
J*f*DI!: this book

Ironically (appropriately?!) this book needed J*f*DI! Following the release
of *Being the Best*, my first book, the biggest demand and request was for
a book specifically on the LifeCompass, which came to be known as
Get a Life. As is often the way with the writing and publication of a
book, much of the process is stop-start: markets are fickle, editors are
distracted and everyone is trying to predict what the reader really
wants. Proposals come and go and sit in in-trays and in-boxes. A
publisher seems keen and then their mind is changed as some other
book accelerates up a best-seller list. Consequently as an author it
seems at times you are the last person to know what is going on. But
eventually I got the go-ahead for *Get a Life,* from my publisher, and so
sat down to writing and working my plan. I had about five months to
complete its writing: a tight but not unreasonable schedule and one
which I could work around my workshops and speaking engagements.

In the background a book had been coming to fruition in my head
about getting change to really happen: that was J*f*DI! Just Do It! Or
how to get personal change to happen on the big desires. So I sent off
a few proposals. Again as is often the way – and you writers out there
will recognise this – nothing happened as the proposals slipped into
publishing black-holes. And then some encouraging signs and then
nothing. And then stop-start. And then I made contact with How To
Books. And within a few days we were on. However, there was a
challenge: to get it to market for our deadline. I had just one calendar
month! And I had some workshop commitments I would not be able
(or actually wish to) change. Well, what a great opportunity to use the
J*f*DI! strategy? How did I apply J*f*DI!?

Step 1: Give ATTENTION at BRAIN level
Adjusting your mindset to support your change

As you know, mindset drives our behaviour. And our behaviour will drive our results. With a tough deadline such as this, if we begin to feel we can't do it, then we will be distracted by our concerns. If we aren't able to stay focused then we will lose our creativity. So, key mindsets for me were:

- **I can.** I recognised and accepted that I had met tough deadlines before and had been able to meet them. I believed that with some careful planning I could clear some immersion time from my diary.
- **This is a great opportunity.** I realised this was a great opportunity to describe the use of JfDI! JfDI! was a strategy that I used all of the time, but here was an opportunity I could document. I knew that readers always like plenty of examples: here would be another great one. I also realised that many journalists, quite rightly, like to probe the author's real experience. This too would create an appropriate anecdote.
- **Whatever happens it'll be great learning.** I decide to view it as a great opportunity to see firstly how far JfDI! could be stretched as a methodology and secondly how my writing skills could be developed. And were I to miss the deadline, I certainly would have learnt a lot.

Step 2: Give ATTENTION at EMOTION level
Getting passionate and creating a vivid, explicit, mental model

My personal vivid, explicit, mental model for this book was already well established. It had been in my proposal, it had been reviewed many times in my discussions with potential publishers. I was regularly thinking about it. I often up-dated the model following its use on a workshop. My VEMM was well on the way, but as with all of us, it needed bringing sharply into focus.

It had certainly got a little 'fuzzy' because of no and/or cautious responses from some publishers. After several hours work over a couple of days in parallel with early background writing, VEMM slipped fully into focus and I had my impetus. I now knew exactly what it was I wanted to create. As many teachers and writers will agree, once you start having to explain your ideas in detail, you soon get a clear vision.

Step 3: Give ATTENTION at STRATEGIC level
Selecting strategies to guarantee success

Having written a couple of non-fiction books I felt I had a pretty good strategy. These strategies were based on early initial guidelines from authors such as Natalie Goldberg and Julia Cameron. A key element of their advice was to get on with the task and not to procrastinate. In particular stop feeling that there is any thing 'special' about your art-form, in this case writing. The more we feel 'precious' about what we are trying to do, the more we look for particular environments, circumstances and situations in which to do our writing, all of which are often increasingly elusive, the less likely we are to get any actual writing done. I believed that was still the basis of my writing strategy. I had found it helped me, it worked and it was productive. It also worked particularly well with my views on 'flow state', meditation and peak productivity (discussed elsewhere, particularly in *Being the Best*).

I took a bit of time out to reflect on (1) what I could learn from my last writing sessions on my second book, *Get a Life* and (2) what would be particularly important for me given that my writing time was going to be so truncated (when applying a strategy to our personal circumstances, it is always useful to check whether there are any reasons why you are not able to use the strategy as the original practitioner encouraged its use). Critical here is that I like to have 'reflection time' where I leave a section of the book for a few days so that ideas can begin to 'knit together' and key insights can then be put across to the reader in the most elegant way. I decided that I would use some of my work-out time in the gym for this. Particularly when I am running a workshop or writing book, I like to workout to ensure maximum energy. But there is also the potential of think time: I used that. This worked well and I felt I was able to fully 'run' my excellence strategy.

Step 4: Give ATTENTION at TACTICAL level
Getting tactical to ensure vision into action

So my overall strategy was pretty simple: put the hours in and the quality will arrive; the one I have always used, plus a few refinements based on my own leanings. But I needed to recognise that the hours were more limited than usual and that I would need to be particularly clever on getting my reflection time.

Tactics I particularly employed were:
- Changing the structure of my writing day. Normally I like to be working on a couple of books and/or articles at one time. When time pressure is not too great, I find the change of materials useful for sparking ideas. However in this case, I felt the critical issue was not getting ideas formulated for new material (I felt I had achieved that) but getting this book written.
- Making a checklist of anything I could delay for this short period, things which I might normally have done in a piecemeal way. There was workshop preparation for example. All were moved to a later part of my diary.

Step 5: Create IMMERSION at BRAIN level
Getting resourceful

Inclination to act was more critical than ever. Prolonged periods of writing must not feel as if they have become a duty, otherwise it is painful for the author and the reader will sense the fatigue. I ensured my state was peak by continuing to go to the gym; with the time pressure it would have been easy to decide not to go and also to be particularly aware of how I might be feeling and to expect some periods of intense frustration because of lack of time – and certainly I had those! The important thing was to work through them and keep the process going: love the dip and love the plateau! Everything I could put off for one month I did. This was a pleasurable thing to do, because I knew that I would have made a huge leap forward with my writing by achieving this book.

I took particular care on the immersion week to ensure that I ate well and got enough sleep. As I have stressed several times, getting the personal change we seek can be as demanding as an athlete wanting to give their best performance.

Step 6: Create IMMERSION at EMOTION level
Using the pain/pleasure lever

I knew that the lever was going to be important. The challenge with any kind of immersion phase is getting the balance between the prolonged change and simple boredom, brain fatigue and lack of 'freshness'. The pain/pleasure lever was important.

I made these all absolutely explicit. Key on pleasure was the benefit of getting my ideas that have been developed over many years of running workshops to a wider audience. The biggest potential pain was (1) missing the key date in the year which was most important for us and secondly (2) not having been able to implement JfDI! The key pleasures considered were having been able to add another successful book to my portfolio and to have illustrated how well the JfDI! strategy can work.

Step 7: Create IMMERSION at STRATEGIC level
Break and date

For this process, I broke down everything I could and perhaps more than usual. Thus: writing sessions were 90 minutes followed by a 10 minute stretch and 30 minutes edit/review. I attempted to cycle these through the day with a couple of mediation periods in there as well. As mentioned above, gym sessions were maintained as were regular walks. Keeping up normal human activity was vital: family life continues! The overall book was created as an outline to what I wished to create and then various sections were allocated target numbers of words. Each day had a daily writing target, with 'percentage success' so far.

Step 8: Create TACTICS at IMMERSION level
Commit to plan

The wall planner was there in front of me: no confusion as to what was expected of me! In particular for my immersion week, no external appointments were accepted. Key milestones were flagged in a variety of colours – milestones in quantity (i.e. number of words) and quality (edited and proofed) to my satisfaction.

Step 9: Create MOMENTUM at BRAIN level
Pareto Power

There were many things I could have done with a 12-month run-up to this work. But I identified what were the Pareto factors for this much shorter delivery time:
- Deliver the number of words agreed, on the subject agreed.
- Deliver against the quality targets of differentiated book and style with key insights .
- Produce great practical explanatory text.
- Create a great cover.

In all our discussions, we kept coming back to those areas of attention. In all my work, I continued to focus on what was needed of me.

Step 10: Create MOMENTUM at EMOTION level
Breaking the pattern

An initial major pattern interrupt was as follows: to get a great feeling of initial success and start with such an initially daunting task, I decided that I would write across the whole book, rather than chapter by chapter building up as I normally do. This was a very helpful initial interrupt on previous practice as it did give encouragement that progress was being made, and rapidly.

I used every pattern interrupt I needed. Whenever I found either quantity (i.e. targeted number of words per day) or quality (working to the high level of insights and clarity I require) were slipping, I used a pattern interrupt such as:

- Blast of great music
- Change of location for working
- Write on paper for a short while away from the screen and then type up.

Step 11: Getting a STRATEGY at MOMENTUM level
Breaking through

Undoubtedly the biggest potential blockers were (1) fear: had I simply taken on too much? And (2) potential chaos: life needed to carry on while the book was being written.

Both blockers were specifically addressed.

Step 12: Bold first steps
Take it away!

What bold steps did I take? The simplest and the biggest was to agree to do it to that deadline! At one stage I had a half-hour period when I really considered that I had taken on too much. The second was to immediately start writing and get a significant number of words done.

The book was delivered to the standards we wanted and I hope you are enjoying it and finding it helpful!

I promise you: JfDI! does work! Now: go to it!

Chapter 7
JfDI!: the basis of organisational and cultural change

If creating change at an individual level at times proves daunting, cultural and organisational change often seems a potential nightmare and close to an impossibility. Here's how JfDI! helps:

Introduction

The basis for all organisational and cultural change is with the individual. No number of 'launches', 'roll-outs' or 're-orgs' will suffice unless that connection to the individual is made. No team, no division, no organisation can change unless individuals are willing to change. And often they are not or their willingness is as short-lived as their own personal desire to learn a language, for example. And that is why much organisational and cultural change is at best painfully slow and at worst a miserable impossibility.

Why don't individuals want to change?

Because 'now sort of works'. Because 'I don't trust you after the fiasco of last time'. Because 'I don't see why I should change for the common good, when I don't seem to be getting any personal salary increase from the common rewards'. Because 'I can't be bothered'. Because 'I'm confused with the various messages which I am getting'.

Because, in general although the logic of change is there, although there are reasons for change, the emotional aspect, the 'buy-in', the trust is very much not there.

So when we need change in an organisation, how do we get it?

And of course we do need change. Here is not the place to quote the impressive array of statistics which remind us how great the rate of change is out there. And you'd need to be a true Luddite to believe that it is not going to affect you, because it is affecting you already. It's the bank manager scenario. The bank manager scenario?

There was a time in the UK, perhaps some 20 or 30 years ago. A time when mobile phones were very special and very rare. When 'fax' was hardly a twinkle in someone's eye and having your own land-line on your desk was still a status symbol for many. And in UK banks, bank managers made decisions about all the important things: about your loan, your mortgage, even about whether to allow you an account. Were you after all the 'right' kind of customer? And many bank managers had done such a job for the majority of their career; perhaps 40 years or more. And then it all came to an end. Computerisation. Stiffer competition. Consumer choice. And naturally the role of the bank manager went with it. And now on the rare occasion when you would appreciate speaking personally to 'someone senior in the bank', you find there is no one. Just a remote administrator at district level.

That's the bank manager scenario. And it is being played out at every level for every market, for every organisation, for every role. And that is why we need change.

AIM 4 BEST at organisational level

To create change at organisational level, we change our focus, apparently paradoxically, from 'the organisation', this 'amorphous blob', to the individual. A person with thoughts and feelings. And importantly the person who will be most affected by the change and will ensure the change is effected (or not, of course). And we do it through our strategy: *AIM 4 BEST*. Let's take a look at how we use Attention, Immersion and Momentum, but now we do it from the perspective of the organisation, not simply the individual.

Attention

Everyone in the organisation must know this is serious, everyone must
be bought-in. It is not just something to concern the 'exec team'. Of
course initial planning, ideas and initial exploration of concepts are
very much the role of the exec team. That is after all what they are
paid to do. No, once change is on it must be done comprehensively.
Get everybody involved. And remember you don't get attention by
being half-hearted, so don't be. The half-day fun event, the one-day
course at which the senior teams supposedly bond through some
rafting exercises: these are not enough. You must work specifically at
the four levels of change: brain level, emotional level, strategic level
and tactical level, for every single person if change is to be secure and
sustained. Once you have attention (and we will look at an example in
a moment), you must move to the next stage, which is of course:

Immersion

There is so much going on in an organisation, so to wire it in fully, we
must get immersion. If not, the initiative will be splintered, there will
be insufficient notice taken to get the critical change, to cause the
tipping point which will ensure it happens. Once again, such
immersion must be done at the four levels of change.

Momentum

And then of course, can the organisation maintain this change process?
Can it create momentum behind this initiative which has been
designed. Can it follow through? Momentum is the stage when we
ensure that this is more than just an initiative to meet some director's
individual brief. That this is something real.

Attention, Immersion, Momentum. Each phase, as you now well
know, requires work at four levels. These levels must be implemented
at all individual levels. We'll take a very simple example: a new
customer service initiative.

Example: New customer service initiative

The scenario: feedback from customers has revealed that the perception of the majority of customers is that service levels are simply not high enough.

How **not** to do it.

- Announce a new initiative at the annual kick-off with some clever branding and a logo. Plug it in retrospectively to the competency scheme. *We are all easily seduced by the 'action' of initiatives and by spending money. Such brandings and kick-offs are ideal for such seduction and have the added advantage that there is plenty which is visual to see and the initiator of the scheme can point to what he/she has done.* <u>In general avoid this approach.</u>

- Arrange a certain number of trainings. *A 'training' or 'course' has been seen since the earliest existence of the organisation as an excellent way to create change. And it can do. But those on the training do need a receptive mindset and there must be continued follow-through. There rarely is.* <u>In general avoid this approach.</u>

- Delegate it down to the front-line junior levels; after all they are the ones who speak to the customers. *They are the ones doing it so they are the ones who need to be accountable. Unfortunately they find they are typically stymied in their ability to realise their objectives because of behaviours which still exist at senor levels.* <u>In general avoid this approach.</u>

- Evaluate the programme in a spurious way. *It is easy to create success metrics. Measure the number of people who attended a change and transition programme. Measure the number of accounts who have been visited to explain the new initiative. But these are not measuring the success of the change. They are simply measuring things and/or activities.* <u>In general avoid this approach.</u>

- Move on to a new initiative. *When it really is apparent that little has been achieved through the initiative, so it becomes time to distract and 'gee people up' again through a new initiative.* <u>In general avoid this approach.</u>

OR

- Send out a long e-mail to everyone in the organisation explaining how things need to change. *43% won't read it. 27% will read it and ignore it. 19% will think it's good but await further instructions. 11% will be the keen, natural change agents, but they will find it hard going without much internal support.* In general avoid this approach.
- Wrap the e-mail up in a lot of jargon language about 'securing the sector envelope in a cocoon of trust'. *And those you might have won over will think 'bullshit'. And they are are right.* In general avoid this approach.

OR

- Launch the customer value set, and ask everyone to live by a list of values headed by integrity. *Values are one of the many tools of change which cannot 'be launched'.* In general avoid this approach.

How **actually** to do it.

Recognise that
- organisational change is dependent upon individual change;
- individual change requires change to be addressed in three phases and each phase at four levels.

Step 1: Mindset for attention

We're looking at an organisational mindset: a mindset which is collective. A set of fundamental beliefs which are essential to the change agents in the organisation:
- We can get collective buy-in to these ideas.
- We can shift entrenched mindsets.
- We can shift the mindsets of individuals, even those who have been here for a great many years.
- We do need to work in some different ways from those in which we have been working.

- We must start respecting the individual.
- We must realise we cannot get all of the people to be happy all of the time.

In addition we can work on what might be considered the mindset of the organisation: how we expect the leaders and individuals in the organisation to work. Perhaps with mindsets such as:

- There is no failure, only feedback.
- There is no exclusivity on great ideas.
- There are rights we all possess: some are job related, e.g. that certain data will be available to a certain person by the last Friday of the calendar month, but many are just 'being-human' related. E.g. common courtesy.

If we are serious about long-term, continuous, sustainable change in an organisation:

1. Ensure the change agents have an appropriate mindset.
2. Encourage a collective mindset which is supportive of change.

Step 2: VEMM for attention

Probably one of the most powerful tools in our sequence. You know what it's like when the new corporate HQ is being built and the architect's model arrives. That's when people really understand what is going on – for good or bad. It's the aspect which is so often ignored in organisational and cultural change: what exactly is the new world we are aiming for going to look like?

So what is the vivid, explicit mental model of the organisation – at the end of this financial year, in three years' time? This of course needs to be created by those who are driving the organisation. But it must be communicated to all those who are working in the organisation. And it must be vivid. It must be explicit. It must be a mental model which every one carries in their head and buys into.

How is the model created initially? Through focus by the exec team initially. They ideally need to take a half-day retreat to focus on this subject. Let's say there are seven in the exec team. The facilitator guides the group through the VEMM power questions:

- What do you want?
- You are now there. What do you see?
- What do you hear?
- What do you feel?

This is done with people considering the questions individually. They then share their thoughts in pairs, then fours (in this case a four and a three) and then as a total team (in this case seven). Why the build-up smaller groupings? So that each individual gets a chance to express their own thoughts and evolve their own thinking through discussion with others, but starting small so that the process gets maximum air-time.

To increase the sophistication of the VEMM process, this process can be repeated within the organisation at various levels and with different roles and departments.

How is the model communicated? Ideally in a dedicated session. And in that dedicated session, three phases are explained:
- How the model was created.
- What the model looks, sounds and feels like.
- How the model will be implemented.

Step 3: Strategy for attention

What is the overall strategy for improving customer service? What do organisations who are good at this stuff do?

Clearly, we need a strategy. Fortunately good strategies for customer service are well understood and increasingly well documented. It's the implementation of them which is the challenge, particularly of the subtle nuances.

Let's illustrate a few points from an outstanding customer service strategy. Remember our goal is slightly different in this section from when we were working on our seven desires. Here we are more concerned about how we use *AIM 4 BEST* for creating change at organisational level, not so much for the specific strategy.

Strategy aspect 1: Everyone is the customer. That means everyone, within the organisation too.
Strategy aspect 2: Essentially the customer is always right, apart from their displaying inappropriate behaviour.

Importantly, we identify, agree and document our strategy.

Step 4: Tactics for attention

Once we have our strategy, once we have an overall process for the initiative, we then must break it down into manageable parts, into our tactics for change.

And we must break this down into what it means for every individual in the organisation. Particularly for the originators of this plan it might seem very obvious what is meant by 'value the customer'. But what does that mean at every level? What does it mean for the receptionist? What does it means for the person who heads up European IT support?

Step 5: Mindset for immersion

OK, so we have attention. That was tough given everything which is going on in an organisation. But we did it. We got attention at brain level, at emotional level. We created an overall strategy and we have developed the tactics which are necessary.

But now we need to push this change: we need to push it so that it becomes part of the organisation. We now enter the immersion phase amd the first level of that.

This, as you will remember, is concerned with creating a mindset which is inclined towards action. The organisation must be made a healthy organisation. Part of this healthy organisation will depend upon the mindset which is adopted and encouraged (see step 1) but it will also be dependent upon what is done at a physical level. Encourage good working areas: space and light. Encourage good working practices: taking proper breaks, eating lunch away from your desk. Encourage health. When an organisation is physically and mentally healthy, there is an inclination towards action.

Step 6: Emotion for immersion: pain/pleasure

With a healthy inclination toward action, we can then move towards using our lever: our pain/pleasure lever.

To ensure focus in the organisation, all should go through the pain/pleasure question in their individual levels. On an individual level, at a team level and at an organisational level. This is critical. Normally change programmes – quite rightly – focus on the benefits. Here we do focus on those, but we also focus on the problems if those changes are not effected, are not carried out.

When an individual has truly reflected on the costs of not changing, then they will be more of a volunteer than a victim.

Step 7: Strategy for immersion: break and date

We must now break and date what needs to be done. Every strategic thought, every strategic action must be broken down into initially team friendly and then individual friendly chunks. Every tactic which we have originated must be broken down.

Step 8: Tactics for immersion: calendar/diary

These now need to go into the company diary. This company diary is on public display: all are watching and observing. At any key company event, the diary is reviewed for progress and set-backs. All team leaders and individuals should note their individual aspects of the diary. In company meeting rooms, in canteens, the calendar is displayed and progress is noted and celebrated.

Step 9: Mindset for momentum: pareto

In creating the change, we ensure that particularly at organisational level, particularly at divisional and team level, we focus on what is critically important. We ask, what is the 20% which will get us the breakthrough? Thus in customer service perhaps it is getting back to the customer, perhaps it is simply allowing them to get through, perhaps it is recognising that we have simply gone too far with the implementation of our web-based interface.

Step 10: Emotion for momentum: pattern interrupt

We illustrate to the organisation that this is not just another initiative/fanfare which won't amount to anything. That this will actually occur. And the reason for that is breaking old patterns and introducing some new ones.

For example, new customer service initiative: the exec team finally start living and breathing these benefits, rather than just talking about them.

Step 11: Strategy for momentum: blockers

What might block us? As always, consider the benefit of where we are now. And one benefit of now is that we're currently not making the time and money investment which needs to be made: especially time. So how can we overcome that blocker?

For example, we believe the new customer service initiative will reduce our overall cost of attracting and retaining new customers so 'forward invest' using that data to allow us to take on someone to enable us to free up necessary initiative implementation time.

Step 12: Tactics for momentum: 1st step

Decide the first steps. Make them clear and bold. Take them. Announce them and make them happen.

For example, new customer service initiative. Double the numbers manning the hot-line from a certain date. Make it happen on that date with the full numbers and ensure it doesn't have negative implications elsewhere. Report the successes.

Chapter 8
JfDI!: a way of life

JfDI! is an approach, a methodology. It is a philosophy. It is an approach to life that allows you to realise your dreams.

Getting your dreams to happen need no longer be down to 'luck' or something that solely happens to other people. It needn't be a source of constant frustration that just as you get one thing sorted out in your life, another aspect unravels.

Having a wish, a dream, a desire, a goal is now something you can seriously consider and if you wish, get it to happen. To order, on time. And if you are a leader or manger or coach, you can help others to realise their wishes. And if you are a parent you can help your children realise their dreams.

Because, ultimately, JfDI! is a decision. Take that decision. JfDI!

How To Books are available through all good bookshops, or you can order direct from us through Grantham Book Services

Tel: +44 (0)1476 541080
Fax: +44 (0)1476 541061
Email: orders@gbs.tbs-ltd.co.uk

Or via our website

www.howtobooks.co.uk

To order via any of these methods please quote the title(s) of the book(s) and your credit card number together with its expiry date.

For further information about our books and catalogue, please contact:

How To Books
3 Newtec Place
Magdalen Road
Oxford OX4 1RE

Visit our web site at

www.howtobooks.co.uk

Or you can contact us by email at info@howtobooks.co.uk